Poverty
& Labour
——IN LONDON——

Poverty
& Labour
——— IN LONDON ———

Interim Report of a Centenary Survey

Peter Townsend
with Paul Corrigan and Ute Kowarzik

Survey of Londoners' Living Standards No. 1

Published by the Low Pay Unit, in conjunction with
the Poverty Research (London) Trust, June 1987.

First published in 1987 by the Low Pay Unit, 9 Upper Berkeley Street, London W1H 8BY, in conjunction with the Poverty Research (London) Trust

ISBN 0 905211 33 2

Cover and text design: Jan Brown Designs, London
Typeset, printed and bound by Russell Press Ltd, Bertrand Russell House, Gamble Street, Nottingham NG7 4ET

Cover photograph: Raissa Page/Format

Photographs: page 3 John Sturrock/Network, page 7 Michael Ann Mullen/Format, page 12 Brenda Prince/Format, page 30 Sheila Gray/Format, page 45 Raissa Page/Format, page 59 Brenda Prince/Format, page 64 Raissa Page/Format, page 73 Jenny Matthews/Format, page 82 John Sturrock/Network.

The Authors

Peter Townsend is Professor of Social Policy at the
University of Bristol. His seminal work, *Poverty in the
United Kingdom*, has provided the starting point for
most discussions of poverty since its publication.
Paul Corrigan has written extensively on welfare and
education and is involved in the development of
planned economic policies to alleviate poverty.
Ute Kowarzik has worked in labour market research
for the past six years, specialising in the relationship
between gender, employment and opportunity.

Contents

Preface   1

1 Introduction   3

2 Why do We Start with the Role of the
   Labour Market?   7

3 Unemployment and London's Labour Market
   in the 1980s   12

4 Social Polarisation and Trends in Deaths
   in the 1980s   30

5 The Growth of Poverty and the Inadequacy of
   Benefits   45

6 The Feminisation of Poverty   59

7 The Rich, the International Labour Market
   and Poverty   64

8 Alternative Anti-Poverty Strategies   73

9 Conclusion   82

Appendix 1 Deprivation   85

Appendix 2 Poverty   95

Appendix 3 Changes in Household Disposable
            Income of Rich and Poor   102

Appendix 4 Ranking of 755 Greater London Wards
            on a Multiple Deprivation Index   103

References   129

Preface

This is the first of a series of reports on a major survey of Greater London. The survey is in fact the third survey of London life and labour. The first was Charles Booth's pioneering study in the 1880s and 1890s, of which his first book, on East London, was published in 1889. The second was a repeat survey carried out during the worst period of the depression of the 1930s. A series of books, edited by H. Llewellyn Smith, was published in the mid-1930s. Both these major studies sought to establish the extent of poverty in the city and the role of the labour market in bringing about or sustaining such poverty.

In a series of papers and books our new study in the 1980s is intended to do the same. In half-a-century the nature and structure of employment in London has changed radically and in important ways has set the pace for changes taking place in the country as a whole. Starting in late 1985 and extending into early 1987 three sets of information have been gathered: reports on (i) interviews with a random sample of 2700 adults, representing the population of 5,545,000 adults living in Greater London; (ii) interviews with random samples of over 400 adults living in each of two London boroughs — a rich borough, Bromley, and a poor borough, Hackney, so that local as well as regional employment experience can be examined in greater depth; and (iii) interviews with employers in Bromley and Hackney to obtain their views, experiences and predictions.

This book sets the scene for a series of specialised reports. It looks at the latest trends in unemployment, earnings, health and social security revealed by Government statistics, and uses case studies from early interviews in 1985 and 1986 to illustrate developments in London's living standards. It does not report the measured results from the three sample surveys described above. They will be the subject of later reports in 1987 and 1988.

We wish to record our gratitude to the Greater London Council for making this research possible and for believing that the results would be of value to Borough Councils in London and central Government as well as Londoners generally after the abolition of the Council in March 1986. Michael Ward, the former Deputy Leader of the Council and Chair of the GLC Employment and Industry Committee, encouraged the idea for the research and continued to back it unwaveringly, as did the former Director of the Employment and Industry Branch, Robin Murray, and Irene Brueghel, who took charge of the administration and chaired the Steering Committee during the early stages of the programme.

We are indebted to those London residents and employers providing information about their own experiences and circumstances, as we are to interviewers in the Survey Services Division of the Intelligence Unit (now the London Research Centre of the LRB) under John Chapman and Jenny Owen for their difficult and demanding work, especially during the hard winter of 1985-86. Thanks for preparatory or analytical work are due to Jeanette Mitchell, John Mason, Peter Shepherd, Hywel Davies, Ian Longhurst, Gill Courtney, Adrian Wood, Margaret Thomas, Meghnad Desai, Robin Jenkins, Mark Dunn and Margot Halse, and for the initial steps in data processing to the late Ken Stonebank and Iris Belli and their colleagues. A lot of help and encouragement has been provided by the Poverty Research (London) Trust: Adrian Sinfield, Alan Walker and Hilary Rose. We must also record thanks to the Low Pay Unit for their administrative and statistical help during a difficult period of 1986 and especially to Chris Pond, Jill Sullivan and Paige Mitchell.

February 1987

1.

Introduction

The third survey of poverty and the London labour market began in late 1985 and is due to be completed during 1987. Every day interviewers have been bringing back evidence of severe deprivation among the population of 6½ millions. There are people who are homeless and even some, early in 1986, who were sleeping in the open at the end of one of the hardest winters of this century. There are disabled and elderly people too poor to keep the heating on during the day and too frightened to walk the surrounding streets on their own. There are unemployed people whose desperation to keep their families fed and clothed is acute. There are increasing numbers of people earning low pay in bad or thoroughly unsatisfactory working conditions.

Yet these were precisely the concerns of the books being written about the London of 1886. It was on April 17 of that year that Charles Booth established his Board of Statistical Research and began his huge survey of Life and Labour in London, which was to be published eventually in a total of 17 volumes. (The first volume on East London was published by Williams and Norgate in 1889 and a revised edition of 17 volumes by Macmillan in 1902.) In May 1886 Booth delivered his first paper on these interests to the Royal Statistical Society ('Occupations of the People of the United Kingdom, 1801-1881,' Journal of the Royal Statistical Society, 1886).

1886 had been an eventful year. In February there was a riot by the unemployed, driven, according to one historian, by hunger and desperation (Stedman-Jones G., Outcast London, 1972, p.345). In that year Beatrice Webb began her work on the 'sweated' trades of London. Students who came to her account in the heady days of post-war 'full' employment in the 1950s and 1960s believed these trades were an evil which had long since been banished.

Developments in forms of employment in the city in the late 1970s and 1980s have proved them wrong.

During the depression years of 1929-1932 a second survey of London designed to examine the changes that had taken place since Booth's day was carried out (Llewellyn-Smith H., ed., New Survey of London Life and Labour, 1932). The two surveys were a response to grim conditions in London's history. They represented faith in the power of knowledge to move people to change policies. Both were succeeded some years later by substantial anti-poverty measures which have been interpreted in later years as establishing and confirming a 'Welfare State'. There is little doubt that the patient compilation of evidence about economic and social realities contributed positively, by influencing scientific and political opinion, to the changes that were eventually made in policy.

Our work is carried out within that tradition. We believe it is necessary to gather together empirical evidence about working and social conditions in our capital city. Like Booth, we believe it is necessary because there are sections of the population who are not aware that anything is wrong with those conditions or do not believe there are problems of consequence, and are implicitly or explicitly condoning developments which are liable to do even greater harm to society in the future than they are doing at the present. We consider such people are out of touch with events for reasons which may not always be their own fault. Whenever there is a major conflict in any society about how to deal with its internal problems there is always the possibility of insisting on making observations and measures of those problems so that the rift in perceptions of the problems at least might be bridged. Also like Booth we advocate a painstaking approach to the documentation of information about the lives of people, in this case by interviewing a representative sample of the population, so that the work carries conviction and authority with specialists as well as with the public at large. When our work is complete we will be able to describe and analyse the lives of London's people with some considerable confidence.

The London Survey — Summary of Methods

By any reckoning the problems of poverty, unemployment and multiple deprivation have become huge and deserve careful scientific examination. The surveys in London are aimed at illuminating contemporary discussion of all three. We are interviewed a general sample of the adult population of the city; a total of 2700 people have been interviewed at considerable length. Addresses were chosen at random from 30 wards selected at regular intervals from the total of 755, ranked by the index of multiple deprivation that we discuss below. All the adults at each of these addresses were invited to answer questions about employment, income and experiences of, as well as attitudes towards, deprivation. We are also undertaking research in depth in the boroughs of Hackney and Bromley, representing, as demonstrated in the pages above, the impoverished and prosperous ends of the London spectrum. In that stage of the research we invited cross-sections of the borough populations to furnish an extensive job history, as well as comment on the local labour market and other immediately local conditions. And at this stage also information will also be sought from employers in those boroughs so that a better theory of institutional developments can be built up.

This study was not simply carried out within the confines of a University or Polytechnic department, with some input from the GLC thrown in. It was important from the beginning that the whole methodology was discussed fully with all of those who had some important input to make. Thus the Women's Committee Support Unit, the Disability Resources Unit, the Ethnic Minorities Unit and the Industry and Employment Branch of the Greater London Council were all actively involved. This made the research a lot more representative of different interests in London, and also more accountable for the direction it took. Certain approaches and sets of questions depended heavily on this advice; and the combined knowledge and experience of these groups went into the specifics of the questionnaire. At no stage did we feel any intellectual freedoms were curtailed in any way. All the decisions about the form and content of the surveys rested finally with the research team. More positively it must be acknowledged that such inputs enrich the form and nature of social studies such as our own.

It was equally important that our study had to begin within a clear scientific and theoretical framework. As we explain in the next section, we chose to look at living standards in relationship to the labour market. We also chose to study living standards across the board. While much of what we have to say will inevitably concentrate upon the poorer sections of London's society, we have data about and are interested in the rich and people with middle incomes as well and the institutions which govern and afford opportunities in their lives. Although such people may be separated by wealth and location from the poorer people of London, they are inextricably linked through the networks of economic and social organisations and relationships of the capital city. Fundamentally the poor can be understood and their numbers explained not only according to the ways by which they but also the rich actually earn their wealth and live their lives. Of course we recognise this is a proposition which itself requires substantiation and explanation throughout our analysis.

Our study also calls into question many of the 'taken for granted' categories of social life. For example, within this interim report we put considerable emphasis on the problem of 'unemployment'. The question of who is and who is not unemployed has become an issue of considerable political importance. The Government has changed the precise definition (now 19 times) since 1980 — which has had a marked effect upon the numbers officially recognised as unemployed. This study allows the numbers produced by different definitions to be compared. It also allows estimates to be made of the numbers in the population who are not doing any work because they have given up expecting the possibility of labour — for example, many women and older people. While our study can properly reflect what are the official definitions of social relations it can also demonstrate how far the 'official' fails to come to grips with the 'real'.

2.

Why do We Start with the Role of the Labour Market?

For Charles Booth the explanation of poverty was straightforward. It appears in the title of his work and is represented on nearly every page thereafter. His interest is in the life and LABOUR of London's poor. Towards the end of the last century it was obvious to most observers that any understanding or analysis of poverty had to begin with an explanation of the role of the labour market. People were poor because of their lowly position in the labour market. That position was inextricably intertwined with personal and family insecurity, bad housing and poor health. The relationship with the labour market was the key to any complex and satisfactory analysis of poverty.

Booth's work demonstrated this relationship for countless households, ensuring that neither poverty nor the labour market could be considered except in conjunction with the other. It is true that he went on to suggest that the structure of the labour market and of other institutions depended on the efforts, ingenuity and character of individuals making up the population rather than the other way round. As an industrial entrepreneur he was undoubtedly influenced by the theories of the classical economists and was not inclined to look for the blame for society's ills among its primary institutions and elites. Otherwise it is difficult to comprehend his derogatory account of the poorest classes (as for example in the conclusion to the 17th volume of the 1902 edition of

'Life and Labour in London', where he writes of the 'lowest class ... consisting so largely of the inefficient and the worthless' and goes on to advocate compulsory committal to industrial communities like the old workhouses: Booth, 1902, pp.207-208). But he emphatically reaffirmed the connections between poverty and the labour market and for the next 50 years any social or economic explanation of poverty in London had to come to terms with that relationship, the importance of which he had established so convincingly. The work of Booth and his associates, but also of Bowley, Llewellyn-Smith, Ford, Tout and others who highlighted the same relationship in subsequent years, powerfully influenced the policy proposals put forward by successive British governments, particularly during two periods of the formation of the Welfare State, namely 1902-1911 and 1942-48.

However, following the development of welfare benefits after the second world war, poverty as an experience came no longer to be explained so automatically by all and sundry as a consequence of the characteristics and distortions of the labour market. The 1950s and 1960s saw an overall tendency develop among commentators and representatives of government alike to place much more of the blame for poverty on 'natural' or fortuitous adversities like widowhood, sickness and old age, but also on shortcomings in the individual of education, skill and motivation. The problem of financing the range of state benefits and services took pride of place over the re-constitution of the labour market as the major problem confronted by Government in treating poverty. Full employment, longevity and the relative deficiency of the value of family allowances, or what later came to be called child benefit, seemed to have changed the categories of people that were poor. The poverty of different categories of people seemed to have a much more direct and obvious relationship with their state benefits than with the labour market itself.

Therefore, some of the studies of poverty in the post-war years explored the ways in which the state had failed to provide the great majority of the population with income benefits as of right, or even the safety net that Beveridge had appeared to promise. Poverty became a matter for the social policy expert and not just the economist. While much of this interim report reflects this post-war tradition in calling attention to the importance of the nature and level of state benefits for people in poverty, it also reverts emphatically to the former tradition by giving priority in the analysis to the structure and evolution of the labour market.

This study represents an attempt to return in principle to the original network of explanations. The purpose is not simply to try and reproduce the work of Booth, for the London labour market of 1986 and 1987 is very different from that of a hundred years ago. It is to recognise, as he and his associates did, that the corner-stone of any approach to the problems of poverty in London is the nature, and structure, of the labour market itself. The contemporary labour market has played an increasingly obvious direct and indirect role in the distribution of income and life chances for the capital's population. So although one of the prime aims of this study is to chart and describe living standards and life chances as they are experienced in 1986 and 1987, another is to develop both an analysis and a contribution to political strategy which firmly resecures the London labour market at the core of explanations for London's poverty.

The detail of our analysis must await the preparation of the results of the empirical work. However, in this interim report the rationale for concentrating on the labour market deserves to be outlined.

First, as illustrated later, the economy of London interrelates more obviously with poverty than it did 20 years ago. Unemployment, underemployment, low wages, bad conditions at work and a pervasive insecurity more obviously characteristise the social relationships of London than they did in the 1960s. These experiences are also much more recognisably interlinked with the nature and level of state benefits received. A record number of Londoners receive benefits through means tests, that record being reached not only because of the continuing low level of retirement pensions but because of the increase of long term unemployment, together with restrictions in the scope of benefits obtained in adversity by right. In London in 1969 there were 20,700 unemployed people receiving means tested benefits. By 1983 this had grown to 231,700, which is an eleven-fold increase. These figures do not simply reflect an increase in unemployment, rather they show the extent to which the indignity of the means test has been allowed to apply as well to a far larger proportion of the population.

Second, the Conservative Government has since 1979 successfully reinforced the link between levels of benefit and the levels of wages as well as of jobs in the labour market. The rates of benefits have been presented as necessarily subordinate to the lowest wage-levels. And the levels of wages have been similarly presented as necessarily subordinate to the whims of the market. Time and again successive Secretaries of State for Social Services have made speeches attacking the rates of benefit paid by the Department for which they are responsible as 'interfering' with the wages system, and have implicitly suggested that these rates of benefit, especially for people of working age, must be reduced.

More than any other government this century, the Thatcher Government has developed a set of policies which insist on the close interconnection between the structure of the labour market and the levels and availability of state benefits. Wages have to be reduced (in the coded language of the day they have to become 'more competitive') and benefits have to be reduced more substantially (they have to reach a level where 'genuine' incentives to work can be seen to operate). The laissez-faire policies of the 19th Century have been revived and applied to an increasing extent. The assumptions which are adopted, and the conclusions which are drawn from current events by Government ministers may indeed be wrong, but this interconnection between benefits and labour market has been powerfully established in the public domain, and has to be accepted as an undeniable fact.

Third, in another part of the political spectrum and in reaction to the Government's policies, very many local authorities have set up departments aimed at looking at the local economy and if possible uncovering ways of intervening in that economy. Before its abolition the GLC was no exception. Its Industry and Employment Branch developed, in conjunction with the Greater London Enterprise Board, a series of economic policies which attempted not only to save and create jobs but to improve the experience of the conditions of the labour market for Londoners. It became obvious that it was the interventions in this market that were necessary for the improvement of the living conditions of Londoners and as a consequence it was within that GLC department this study of living standards was financed and developed.

Finally, it has become clearer and clearer that the experience of poverty is not simply a matter of a lack of money which policies confined to earnings, taxes and benefits can remedy. Any reconsideration of Booth's work and indeed of the whole tradition of poverty studies demonstrates the concern of social scientists and other observers with the whole gamut of social conditions and relationships — and not just with rates of pay and benefits. Yet it is the limited formulation of the phenomenon which has stuck in the public mind. Of course, much of the research described in these pages and in subsequent reports will be concerned with the financial aspects of poverty and will present a detailed analysis of income levels and disparities. However, in developing and extending different measures of deprivation it will become evident that indicators of the whole quality of life and not just its financial aspects have to be appraised to understand the nature and force of the phenomenon. The labour market is not important simply because it distributes different levels of remuneration in wages and salaries. It plays a major role in many other sets of experiences. The work people do affects their health; their conditions of work will affect their domestic lives and, most importantly in the contemporary context, the insecurities experienced in the labour market affect every part of life. It is the building block of working people's lives. For most Londoners, there is no nest egg to depend upon when 'hard times' come. There is only the ability to work and to gain subsistence and meaning from that work.

For these reasons our research framework both in general methodology and in terms of the specifics of questions asked in the questionnaires opens up the relationship with the labour market.

Therefore, in this introduction to our interim report we want to begin with some of the major themes within the London economy that have helped to create the huge disparity in living conditions of the capital city.

3.

Unemployment and London's Labour Market in the 1980s

In 1987 London's economy is in deeper crisis than it has been for a hundred years. In certain clear respects it is worse than the 1930s. The rigours of those depression years affected other regions more than London and did not bring quite the same extent of misery and insecurity to the capital. There were even areas of what is now Greater London, particularly to the East and West of the city, which actually prospered during that period and which are now in economic decline. During the first five years of the 1930s London's production increased slightly by 13 per cent while that of the rest of the country showed no growth at all. There are indeed areas of London which continue to thrive in the late 1980s but most areas are experiencing harsh economic pressures.

How might present trends be summarised? With over 400,000 unemployed London now has the largest concentration of unemployment of any city of the industrial world (Murray, 1985, p.47). In Europe only Paris and Naples approach these numbers (Eurostat, Yearbook of Regional Statistics, 1985, Table II.8). Britain lost 25 per cent of jobs in manufacturing between 1971 and 1981 but London lost 36 per cent. Jobs melted away more rapidly than at any time in the city's history. Between 1973 and 1982 more than half-a-million jobs were lost in the London economy (GLC, 1985, p.5).

Unemployment has spread swiftly like an industrial contagion. Numbers have more than trebled since the government came to power in 1979 — from 122,000 in 1979 to 408,000 in 1985. This growth, partly explained by Government policies, has inevitably provoked extreme insecurity among the London workforce. Opinion polls demonstrate the growth in numbers of people expressing anxiety about their own and their children's future. Unemployment affects a much wider group of people than those who are unemployed at any one time. Large scale unemployment harms many of those people who are still in work by undermining their dependence upon job security.

Obviously this dependence varies among different sections of the workforce. Unemployment affects some parts of the workforce far more than others. There are structural divisions — between non-manual and manual, skilled and non-skilled, permanent and temporary, public and private sector, manufacturing and service industries, which explain where the axe of redundancy is likely to fall, and fall most quickly. New technology is being developed faster in some occupations than others. Sometimes jobs are decimated and sometimes nearly as many are replaced by that technology. Certain industries have suffered more redundancies than others. In conditions of high unemployment it is workers with no recognised skills who become most vulnerable to loss of jobs and who find it hardest, especially in competition with the increased numbers of skilled workers to be made redundant, to obtain the few alternative jobs around.

The outcomes are not only unevenly experienced within the London workforce. Some areas suffer harshly, others scarcely at all. Even if you have a job, living in a locality where a third or a half of your neighbours are unemployed is likely to have a marked effect upon your own job security. By contrast, you can live in another locality where it is rare to come across someone who is unemployed and you can go to work and experience that work without any thought of job insecurity. In this way the experience of unemployment affects not just the individually unemployed but groups of workers and entire local communities of the capital city.

The disparities in unemployment result from the differences in the effect and timing of the restructuring of the economy of London. As we shall see, manufacturing has halved over the last 15 years, and it was the workshops of inner London that were the first to close. Some boroughs have been virtually denuded of manufacturing firms which employ more than 200 people. In the borough of Hackney there are none.

While the increase in unemployment has been most dramatic since 1979, the changes in the London economy go back much further than that. Both in numbers of jobs and sectors the London economy has changed remarkably over the last three decades. Table 3.1 shows both the overall loss of jobs and the dramatic shift in type of jobs from manufacturing, construction, transport and communications to services, particularly banking, insurance and finance.

TABLE 3.1
Changes in Employment in London, 1951 to 1985 (000s)

Industry Group Standard Industrial Classification (1980)		1951	1971	1981	1981 Sept	1985 Sept
0	Agriculture, forestry	—	—	—	2	3
1	Energy, water supply	—	—	—	56	44
2-4	Manufacturing	1,523	1,049	671	686	572
5	Construction	283	196	163	160	144
	(Distributive trades)	599	525	477	—	—
64-65	Retail distribution	—	—	—	319	327
6 rem.	Wholesaling, hotels and catering	—	—	—	369	386
7	Transport and communic.	420	440	373	371	323
8	Banking, insurance and finance	187	404	463	568	633
91-92	Public admin./defence	317	334	315	370	375
93-99	Education, health etc.	—	392	424	667	665
	(Professional services)	365	508	601	—	—
6-9	All services	2,743	2,622	2,636	2,663	2,709
0-9	All employed	4,288	3,939	3,528	3,567	3,471

Sources: 1951-1981, Census Reports; Sept. 1981-Sept. 1985, Employment Gazette, (Dec. 1983, Table 3 and Jan. 1986, Table 1.5).

During the 1980s the contraction has continued quite fast. 'Between 1981 and 1984, London lost 106,000 jobs but gained 7,000 residents of working age. Unemployment among the remaining residents has increased by 93,000. Vacancies notified to jobcentres increased, but only by 10,000.' (Inner London Consultative Employment Group, London's Labour Market, 1965-1985, 1986, p.1). Manufacturing jobs have continued to decline quite fast. On the other hand, as Table 3.1 also shows, jobs in education and health, public administration and defence, have stayed at about the 1981 levels, and jobs in banking, insurance and finance have continued to increase. Perhaps ironically, for the first time in the history of the capital city, jobs in banking, insurance and finance now exceed by a substantial margin those in manufacturing.

In the next years there is no prospect of much relief in outlook for employment. Up to 1990 at least another 100,000 jobs in manufacturing are expected to be lost (mainly in mechanical, instrument and electrical engineering, and in the manufacture of metal goods), together with a substantial number in construction and the energy industries. Another 150,000 jobs are also expected to be lost from service industries. Big reductions in transport and communication, distributive trades and miscellaneous services will be partly offset by continuing gains in banking, insurance and finance and public administration (GLC, The London Labour Plan, 1986, p.48).

The scourge of unemployment has been highly selective.

Depression has taken hold of certain types of employment and therefore of particular areas where those types of employment were most widely to be found. 'From the second half of the 1960s until the end of the 1970s, London's deindustrialisation was concentrated in inner London and the east. Docklands was particularly severely hit. In the period 1971-78 east London lost more than 20,000 dock jobs and 53,000 manufacturing jobs.... The 1980s have deepened the economic crises in these areas, but they have also seen the spread of similar destruction to West London. In Hayes and Hounslow, Southall and Park Royal, a once thriving economic landscape has become like an industrial cemetery' (GLC, London Industrial Strategy, pp. 6-7). One report countered the myth of West London's continuing prosperity (GLC, The West London Report, 1984). A later report of a public inquiry emphasised the seriousness of the situation and showed that 'the notion of the inner city is an inappropriate concept with which to understand the reasons behind job loss in Greater London. Far more significant for London, and repeatedly in West London, has been the loss of employment and training opportunities due to the actions of multi-national companies who have chosen to close down production in major urban areas and within Britain and transfer production elsewhere in the country or world. For West London, escalating land and property values can also be seen to be reinforcing this loss of manufacturing industry and employment.' (GLC, West London: The Public Inquiry into Jobs and Industry, 1985).

The collapse of industry in London accounts only in part for the high level of unemployment found in deprived localities. These areas contain disproportionately high numbers of people with few educational and publicly recognised vocational skills; few assets, like houses and cars, and few other resources, like close relatives in employment who can introduce them either to vacancies or ideas about possible employment. Some of these areas also have meagre facilities for prospective employers and are regarded as unattractive, except perhaps to those who are in different respects prepared to cut corners or exploit people desperate for work. A rapidly rising level of local unemployment tends to have a multiplier effect, tying many of the residents more firmly to the problems of the local labour market.

The Selective Trends in Unemployment: Localities

By January 1986 the unemployment rate in Hackney was 22.7 per cent and in Tower Hamlets 22.2 per cent, compared with 6.0 per cent in Sutton and 5.9 per cent in Kingston. All these figures would have scandalised a previous generation. In 1963 the Minister for the Developing Regions, (then Quentin Hogg) launched a policy to provide grants to those areas of the country seen as being 'unemployment black spots'. Areas with unemployment rates

TABLE 3.2
Unemployment by Borough

January	Number of unemployed			Unemployment rate		
	Male	Female	Total	Male	Female	Total
City of London	89	30	119	4.8	1.9	3.4
Camden	10,826	4,910	15,736	21.2	10.8	16.3
Kensington & Chelsea	6,696	3,153	9,849	16.3	8.6	12.6
Westminster	9,902	4,178	14,080	18.7	8.9	14.1
Hackney	15,023	5,893	20,916	28.5	15.0	22.7
Hammersmith & Fulham	8,919	3,805	12,724	19.6	9.9	15.1
Haringey	12,265	5,477	17,742	20.8	12.0	17.0
Islington	12,007	4,928	16,935	24.7	12.8	19.5
Lambeth	19,054	7,529	26,583	26.5	13.0	20.4
Lewisham	13,152	5,425	18,577	19.4	10.5	15.5
Newham	12,866	4,798	17,664	21.4	12.0	17.7
Southwark	15,958	5,793	21,751	25.4	12.0	19.6
Tower Hamlets	12,512	3,763	16,275	28.6	12.7	22.2
Wandsworth	11,897	5,124	17,021	15.4	8.3	12.2
Inner London	161,166	64,806	225,972	21.9	11.1	17.1
Barking & Dagenham	6,260	2,543	8,803	14.8	9.3	12.7
Barnet	7,248	4,008	11,256	8.5	6.4	7.6
Bexley	5,551	3,266	8,817	8.5	7.2	8.0
Brent	11,619	5,182	16,801	15.6	9.2	12.8
Bromley	6,816	3,445	10.261	7.7	5.5	6.8
Croydon	9,354	4,679	14,033	9.7	6.7	8.4
Ealing	9,996	5,338	15,334	11.6	8.2	10.1
Enfield	7,318	3,523	10,841	9.3	6.3	8.1
Greenwich	10,786	4,891	15,677	17.3	10.9	14.6
Harrow	4,014	2,349	6,363	6.8	5.6	6.3
Havering	6,406	3,124	9,530	8.9	6.6	8.0
Hillingdon	4,723	2,813	7,536	6.5	5.5	6.1
Hounslow	6,043	3,603	9,646	10.1	8.2	9.3
Kingston	2,602	1,434	4,036	6.6	5.0	5.9
Merton	4,414	2,177	6,591	9.1	6.0	7.8
Redbridge	6,228	3,213	9,441	9.4	6.8	8.3
Richmond	3,272	1,916	5,188	6.7	5.2	6.1
Sutton	3,307	1,954	5,261	6.5	5.3	6.0
Waltham Forest	8,662	3,889	12,551	14.1	8.8	11.9
Outer London	124,619	63,347	187,966	9.9	7.0	8.7
Greater London	285,785	128,153	413,938	14.3	8.6	11.9

Notes
1. Ward based data from Department of Employment.
2. Unemployment rates calculated by the Intelligence Unit as a percentage of the economically active residents taken from the Unit's 1985 projection 3B for the appropriate year.

higher than 3 per cent were to be singled out for subsidies. Public perceptions of what constitutes high and low unemployment have certainly changed.

For men the unemployment rate has been higher and for women lower than the average, as Table 3.2 shows. In 1986 the rate for men in inner London was nearly double that for women — though it should be pointed out that there are more women than men who are not entitled to unemployment and other benefits and so are not officially counted as unemployed. As we will argue below, the real rate of unemployment among women is at least as high as among men, and the lower official rate has been gradually catching up on that for men in the last seven years. In the fifteen years since 1971 the unemployment rate for both men and women has increased both absolutely and proportionately much faster in inner boroughs like Hackney and Tower Hamlets than in outer boroughs like Sutton and Kingston. Table 3.3 picks out the trends. Unemployment has grown in all boroughs, but absolutely and proportionately by more in the deprived inner London boroughs than in the outer boroughs. The 'gap' between boroughs has widened from a ratio of 2.4 to 1 to 3.8 to 1. This differential development has had serious social as well as economic effects, which are still being puzzled over, and there are consequences of the divergent trends too for national policies, which have not yet been properly digested.

The trends can be clarified by applying modern statistical techniques of cluster analysis, principal component analysis and analysis of change, using regressions, to large sets of data, so that departures from 'expected' changes can be picked out. The phenomenon of 'polarisation' can be readily demonstrated for unemployment during 1971-1981, and although not consistently, to some other indicators of deprivation. 'Boroughs with above average unemployment in 1971 (e.g. Hackney and Lambeth) are even more above average in 1981'…'Increased segregation [between boroughs] is particularly apparent in indicators of ethnic status, unemployment and lone parent families for which the regression slope exceeds one. This is indicative of a widening gap between boroughs containing few deprived groups and those containing many.' (Congdon P., Social Structure in the London Boroughs: Evidence from the 1981 Census and Changes since 1971, Statistical Series No. 28, 1984, pp.24 and 25).

The boroughs themselves cover different kinds of areas and the trends become more sharply discernible for smaller areas. When London is divided into wards the selective nature of recent trends in unemployment can be picked out more clearly. In 1981 the unemployment rate in three wards (Crofton in the Borough of Bromley, Selsdon in the Borough of Croydon, and Cheam South in the Borough of Sutton) which lie at one extreme of a continuum from low to high rates of unemployment remained low, at around 2½ per

TABLE 3.3
Changes in Unemployment, London Boroughs (1971-1986)
(Percentage of economically active population)

Boroughs (ranked by 1986 rate)	1971	1981	1986
Hackney	6.6	15.9	22.7
Tower Hamlets	7.5	16.1	22.2
Lambeth	6.1	13.2	20.4
Southwark	6.3	13.1	19.6
Islington	6.2	13.4	19.5
Newham	6.1	13.0	17.7
Haringey	4.8	11.0	17.0
Camden	6.1	11.8	16.3
Lewisham	5.2	10.5	15.5
Hammersmith and Fulham	6.3	11.5	15.1
Greenwich	4.9	9.9	14.6
Westminster	5.8	10.8	14.1
Brent	4.8	10.5	12.8
Barking and Dagenham	4.8	10.0	12.7
Kensington and Chelsea	6.6	10.8	12.6
Wandsworth	5.8	10.4	12.2
Waltham Forest	4.2	9.1	11.9
Ealing	4.1	8.8	10.1
Hounslow	3.3	7.3	9.3
Croydon	3.4	6.4	8.4
Redbridge	3.5	6.8	8.3
Enfield	3.3	6.8	8.1
Bexley	3.5	5.8	8.0
Havering	3.3	6.3	8.0
Merton	3.6	6.3	7.8
Barnet	3.7	6.5	7.6
Bromley	3.3	5.4	6.8
Harrow	3.1	5.6	6.3
Hillingdon	2.9	5.8	6.1
Richmond	3.6	5.7	6.1
Sutton	2.9	4.8	6.0
Kingston	2.7	5.2	5.9
Greater London	4.7	9.0	11.9

Source: For 1971 and 1981: Hollis J, 1981 Census Results for Greater London and the London Boroughs: Small Area Statistics and Historical Comparisons, Greater London Council, 1983, Table 23. For January 1986: London Research Centre.

cent, compared with 1971, while in three wards at the other extreme, namely Ordnance in Newham, Spitalfields in Tower Hamlets and Carlton in Brent, it had already reached 22 or 23 per cent.

The latest estimates for 1986 show a further polarisation. In the 25 most deprived wards of the population of London (accounting for a total of more than 200,000 London residents) the unemployment rate for men and women combined increased from 17.5 per cent to 25.0 per cent, as Table 3.4 shows. The rate in three wards, St Mary's, in Tower Hamlets, Angell in Lambeth, and Liddle in Southwark, substantially exceeded 30 per cent. The male unemployment rate was even higher than the combined rate for both sexes in these wards. In the 25 least deprived wards, similarly accounting for a total number of more than 200,000 residents, unemployment increased from 3.3 per cent to 4.3 per cent. The ratio between the two sets of wards widened from 5.3 to 1 to 5.8 to 1. It can be seen that in some of the least deprived wards, like Woodcote in Sutton, Ickenham in Hillingdon and Headstone North in Harrow, the rate remained static or even declined.

The Selective Trends in Unemployment: Women and Minority Groups

Government data suggest that women in London have suffered lower rates of unemployment than women elsewhere. Early in 1985, for example, the rate for London was 7.6 per cent, compared with 9.8 per cent for the U.K. as a whole. The reason is to be found in the fact that during the 1970s London had more of a development of service, administrative and office jobs than the rest of the country, many of which could be filled by women. In the earlier stages of cut-backs in employment these sectors were less affected by recession and by technical innovation. That situation is now beginning to change rapidly, and is reflected in the relative unemployment rates of the sexes.

It has always been assumed that unemployment 'hurts' men more than it does women. Men, the argument goes, get a great deal more of their self-image and social status from the nature and day to day experience of work. Culturally, when that is withdrawn then they are supposed to suffer most. Indeed, while men make up 60 per cent of the London workforce they make up 70 per cent of unemployed claimants. That result is based on the Government's definition of unemployment. Britain would appear to be the only country in Western Europe where rates of female unemployment are below those for males. The figures for men and for women in the years since 1979 are set out in Table 3.5. In six years the percentage rate for men has nearly tripled, and yet the rate for women has nearly quadrupled. But while in London registered unemployment among women has been catching up on that among men it is still only about two-thirds the men's rate.

However, this difference is more apparent than real. For many years fewer unemployed women than men have registered as unemployed, and in the 1980s fewer have claimed benefit under the procedures for counting the unemployed developed by Government. Fewer women than men qualify for benefit. Therefore even if they go to a job centre they will not be registered as unemployed.

Again, in local conditions of high unemployment and sharp

TABLE 3.4
Number of unemployed — May 1986
Most Deprived and Least Deprived Wards

		Number Unemployed		Per cent Unemployed	
		1981	May 1986	1981	May 1986
Most Deprived					
Spitalfields	Tower Hamlets	658	997	21.4	28.0
St. Mary's	Tower Hamlets	571	1,047	18.7	32.8
Carlton	Brent	709	797	20.9	23.8
Golborne	Kens. & Chelsea	625	889	18.6	25.9
Shadwell	Tower Hamlets	637	938	16.7	23.5
Haggerston	Hackney	507	653	17.3	23.9
Blackwall	Tower Hamlets	556	654	20.7	24.4
St. Katherine's	Tower Hamlets	754	1,181	15.1	19.7
Kings Park	Hackney	667	933	19.1	27.8
White City & Shepherds Bush	H'Smith & Fulham	838	1,285	17.0	26.5
Ordnance	Newham	552	648	22.1	26.7
Angell	Lambeth	1,010	1,918	18.3	36.1
Westdown	Hackney	496	818	18.6	29.9
St. Dunstan's	Tower Hamlets	647	852	17.7	21.5
Liddle	Southwark	974	1,776	18.3	33.7
Harrow Road	Westminster	873	1,212	15.1	20.7
Eastdown	Hackney	712	1,262	16.5	27.7
Queen's Park	Westminster	805	1,013	16.3	20.2
Stonebridge	Brent	561	733	16.5	21.3
Larkhall	Lambeth	1,175	1,721	17.2	24.0
Rectory	Hackney	759	851	18.5	20.8
Avondale	Kens. & Chelsea	611	712	16.4	19.8
Weavers	Tower Hamlets	648	1,045	15.2	23.6
Vassall	Lambeth	1,099	1,571	17.7	24.0
Westbourne	Westminster	824	1,080	15.1	22.8
Total 25 Wards		**18,267**	**26,587**	**17.5**	**25.0**
Least Deprived					
Cranham Heath	Havering	128	176	3.1	4.3
Selsdon	Croydon	132	185	2.6	3.5
Cheam South	Sutton	71	75	3.7	3.9
Woodcote	Sutton	79	73	4.8	2.8
Biggin Hill	Bromley	167	250	3.0	4.3
Farnborough	Bromley	129	215	3.1	4.7
West Wickham North	Bromley	133	183	2.9	4.0
Crofton	Bromley	137	256	2.5	4.5
Emerson Park	Havering	194	229	4.2	4.9
Falconwood	Bexley	60	118	3.2	6.3
Malden Manor	Kingston u Thames	71	87	3.1	3.7
Ickenham	Hillingdon	183	195	3.3	3.3
Petts Wood & Knoll	Bromley	220	342	2.9	4.4
West Wickham South	Bromley	135	186	2.9	3.9
Upminster	Havering	191	226	3.6	4.3
Shortlands	Bromley	160	196	3.6	4.3
Woodcote & Couldson W.	Croydon	227	307	3.2	4.3
North Cheam	Sutton	109	160	3.4	4.9
Worcester Pk. S.	Sutton	85	125	3.0	4.3
Monkhams	Redbridge	183	220	3.8	4.5
B'don & Penhill	Bexley	208	288	4.2	5.8
Pinner West	Harrow	151	174	3.4	3.9
Headstone North	Harrow	205	213	4.3	4.3
Tolworth East	Kingston u Thames	96	146	3.6	5.5
Ardleigh Green	Havering	141	225	3.3	5.1
Total 25 Wards		**3,595**	**4,850**	**3.3**	**4.3**

TABLE 3.5
Registered Unemployed in London (1979-1985)

	Numbers (thousands)			Percentage of economically active		
	Men	Women	Men and Women	Men	Women	Men and Women
1979	96	30	126	4.3	2.1	3.4
1980	117	40	157	5.8	1.9	4.2
1981	196	68	264	8.7	4.3	6.9
1982	238	85	323	10.5	5.4	8.5
1983	259	101	360	11.6	6.4	9.5
1984	266	115	381	11.9	7.2	9.9
1985	278	124	402	12.5	7.8	10.5

Source: Employment Gazette, Department of Employment.

competition for work women are much more likely than men to withdraw from the labour market altogether even when they would prefer to take paid employment. Many find they are pressed or encouraged to remain in traditional economically dependent roles as wives or mothers or, while young, within their parents' homes. All this is a familiar refrain from family history, and there are those who are seeking to revive that refrain today. There are strong pressures upon women not to contemplate employment and, if they become unemployed, to defer to the interests of men in looking for alternative work. But contrary influences have also been at work. Married women have been taking paid employment while their children are still young, and have been completing smaller families sooner. This satisfies them and augments family income. More women have been leaving the parental home before marriage and have settled with partners where both expect to follow a career. And employers have taken advantage of many women's availability to work part-time or at unorthodox hours.

For such reasons more women have entered paid employment in recent decades and are looking for work now. There is a reserve army with an eagerness to take paid work whose size appears to have been repeatedly underestimated. The Census of Population of 1981 provided evidence for London showing that unemployment among women was underestimated by as much as 38 per cent. Other evidence shows that even this figure would be higher, depending on the assumptions made in defining (and accepting) individual readiness to take paid work of different kinds. Equally, the Labour Force Survey of 1981 showed that women represent the same proportion of those actually unemployed (40 per cent) as of those actually in paid employment (also 40 per cent).

TABLE 3.6
Unemployment Among Ethnic Minorities by Age (1981)

		Per Cent Unemployed			
Age	West Indian & Guyanese	Indian, Pakistan & Bangladeshi	Other Minorities	All	All 1985
16-19	37	23	18	19	25
19-24	32	13	10	12	18
25-34	14	10	7	7	12
35-44	7	10	5	5	8
45-55	12	12	4	5	9
55-59	5	17	5	5	11
60-64	—	—	7	7	7

Source: GLC, London Labour Plan, 1986, p.198 (from 1981 Labour Force Survey).

Minority Groups

Britain still fails to maintain reliable information about employment and unemployment among ethnic minorities. Unlike statistics for other groups Department of Employment statistics are not available monthly. However, the 1981 Labour Force survey does provide some illumination. Table 3.6 shows first that in that year unemployment rates among Asian groups were about half as much again as, and among West Indian groups about twice, the average. In the last five years the average unemployment rate has nearly doubled and it may be assumed that the differential between blacks and whites is certainly no less and is likely to be larger. This is implied by the exceptionally large increase in unemployment in London wards known to have a high proportion of the population who are black — like Angell ward in Lambeth and St. Mary's in Tower Hamlets.

Another striking feature of Table 3.6 is the exceptionally high rate of unemployment among young people and especially young people of West Indian descent. A major study of black and white unemployed teenagers in urban areas found that concern over unemployment was equal in both groups and although general distress and depression were slightly more common among whites the psychological health of both groups was 'relatively poor.' The study also showed that both groups, even those with long experience of unemployment, searched hard for work. There is ample evidence that young black people suffer considerable disadvantages in the labour market (Warr P., Banks M. and Ullah P., 'The Experience of Unemployment Among Black and White Urban Teenagers,' British Journal of Psychology, 1985, 76, pp.84-85).

One important explanation for the widening gap between blacks and whites in experience of unemployment is the unrepresentative distribution of employment according to industry. For example, many blacks used to work for little pay in food processing industries in inner London, which have now experienced a dramatic loss of jobs. Again, when London Transport went over to one person bus operation on many routes many bus conductors of West Indian origin were made unemployed. These are only examples of what follows from institutionalised racism when a downturn is experienced in an economy or when technological innovations come to be applied. In disemploying a labour force racism operates as influentially as in employing a labour force.

Another vulnerable minority are people with disabilities. Unemployment among registered disabled is much higher than among non-disabled persons. Despite legislation to encourage the employment of 3 per cent disabled in every workforce successive Governments have failed to enforce that legislation and have condoned a much lower percentage, even in the workforces of public authorities. As a consequence registration itself has become something of a dead letter, and the present Government has been allowing it to depreciate further (See Lonsdale S. and Walker A., 'A Right to Work: Disability and Employment, Disability Alliance and Low Pay Unit, London, 1984).

The Uncounted Unemployed

When explored in detail the developments reported above inevitably contain hints of explanation or theory about the re-structuring of the labour force and the consequential social effects. This must be made more explicit. Unemployment and not just employment is being re-structured. During the 1970s monetarists and neo-monetarists began to argue strongly that some of the so-called unemployed were in fact working; that others were between jobs, were disabled or in fact retired or were otherwise 'unemployable'; and that many women seeking work should be steered back into the home where their efforts should primarily lie. Since 1979 the Government has acted in fulfilment of these beliefs. Nineteen changes had been made by the beginning of 1987 with the effect of reducing the counts of the unemployed. The biggest change was made in October 1982, when registration for work at a Jobcentre, Employment Office or Careers Office ceased to be a condition of entitlement to unemployment benefits except for people under the age of 18. As a consequence the former method of counting the unemployed had to be changed. A new count of 'unemployment', based on benefit office computer records, came into being. This replaced the old count of those on the registers who were 'capable of and available for work.' The old count was itself far from complete as a measure of total unemployment. For example, many people not required to register (who had no entitlement to benefit) did not do so and were omitted from the total, even though they were actively seeking work. During the mid-1980s, the

Unemployment Unit has maintained estimates of unemployment on the basis of the former Government definition, in order to call attention to the omission of some 400,000 to 500,000 from the total.

These changes have had everything to do with beliefs on the part of Government as well as industry about the discipline, redundancies and wage levels of different sections of the workforce necessary to make the economy viable and restore levels of profit. One set of beliefs concerns the qualifications, attitudes and other characteristics of the employed. But a corresponding set concerns the qualifications, attitudes and other characteristics of those who might properly be defined as unemployed and deserve support from the State. This is attracting increasingly detailed Government scrutiny.

There is a contrary, and more scientific, approach to the measurement of unemployment. As in a lot of previous work, the London research team has been finding that there is more unemployment than Government statistics allow. Some of this evidence follows familiar lines. More people say they are actively seeking work than the numbers registered or drawing benefit. We are finding interesting examples of people not counted among the unemployed, whom no one could reasonably deny are available for, and actively seeking paid employment. For example, there is a former scaffolder who has been unemployed for 18 months. For the first 12 months he was entitled to unemployment benefit, based on his previous record of paying national insurance contributions regularly, and of course he was counted in the army of unemployed. But after those 12 months he could only claim supplementary benefit and, because his wife has a low paid job, he found he was not entitled to benefit and therefore he is no longer counted as unemployed.

A post office worker was made redundant at the age of 60 in 1984 and despite getting an occupational pension of moderate size wants part-time work. He told the interviewer about a range of initiatives he had in fact taken to find paid work — including written replies to advertisements, letters of enquiry to possible employers and calls in the hope of getting an interview. He gave an account of his health which demonstrated his fitness for work. He also revealed that he looked after two grandchildren for a total of 18 hours a week and did all the household laundry and ironing in addition. He too is not counted in the official total of unemployed.

Before its abolition the GLC called attention to several groups unrepresented in the official total (GLC, London Labour Plan, 1986, pp.199-203). In addition to the total of 400,000 unemployed London claimants officially admitted there were estimated in June 1985 to be another 64,000 who, like the scaffolder described above, cannot claim benefit. Yet such people are in every way looking for work and are comprehensively 'un' employed. Then there were an estimated 60,000 unregistered unemployed women actively seeking work.

Again, the existence of such a substantial number in every region does not appear to be in doubt, and is supported by all the reports of reputable surveys which have been published. The GLC also made calculations of smaller groups (like men aged 60-65 drawing national insurance benefits) who had been struck out of the count of unemployment by Government decision, and other groups (like those in the Youth Training Scheme and people retired prematurely, as well as disabled people) who would take part-time or full-time paid employment if it were available. There was also evidence that a little under a third of the people in part-time work would have been prepared to work full-time had the opportunity been available. This represents underemployment of a considerable size, equivalent to some 18,000 jobs. Even if some allowance is made for marginal or doubtful instances in this attempt to get close to a 'real' estimate of the unemployed in today's labour market conditions at least 150,000 have to be added to the official total of over 400,000 unemployed in London. A more accurate estimate will be given once the present research is completed.

The Government's own Labour Force Survey produces estimates of unemployment in London which are in fact consistent with these criticisms. Table 3.7 gives information for the surveys of 1984, 1985 and 1986 which put the Government's count of claimants in a new light. The real numbers of unemployed people are plainly much higher than the official count, though the measure inevitably depends on the exact criteria for the definition finally accepted. The true London figure for the unemployed seems to be more than half as many again as the official count, even before any estimate for the

TABLE 3.7
Estimates of Unemployment in Greater London and Britain

	thousands		
Definition of Unemployment	Spring 1984	Spring 1985	Spring 1986
Greater London			
All who would like a job	641	607	645
— excluding those who had not looked for work in last 4 weeks, and not available for work in next 2 weeks	544	491	547
— excluding others not available for work in next 2 weeks	522	459	512
Britain			
All who would like a job	5,405	5,233	5,296
— excluding those who had not looked for work in last 4 weeks, and not available for work in next 2 weeks	4,598	4,459	4,513
— excluding others not available for work in next 2 weeks	4,382	4,218	4,293

Source: Hansard, 27 March 1987, cols. 291-2.

prematurely retired is added, and even before estimates are made of many women at home who would take employment if the opportunities offered.

The research team encountered examples of unemployment other than those quoted above which are even more potent for theory. Some of them destroy the neo-classical and not only monetarist explanations for unemployment, which rest predominantly on individual motivations. We have met people who have searched for jobs repeatedly, have marketable skills and are young. Their accounts are often depressing and turn the locus of cause back to employers, management, Government and international agencies. There is one 21 year old woman living in South London who was educated to the age of 17. She has two good A-levels. She has now been unemployed for 39 months and has wanted work all that time. When asked to describe poverty she said, 'People having no food, no clothes, no future and nowhere to stay. No hope of getting a job and no hope of it getting any better. The welfare system is going downhill: it's going to be made harder for the poorer classes. I fear they are going to take the health service away'. In many respects that 21 year-old woman is a child of her times. The example is not one that the depression of the 1930s would have produced. A generation of young people without work and without any hope of paid work is being created in the 1980s.

The nuances of the meaning and extent of unemployment are not exhausted with these examples. We are doing our best to track, and measure, the unpaid work which many people, especially women, do. It is one of the realities which help us to interpret, and weigh the seriousness of, socially perceived employment and unemployment. Many women have highly responsible, and often extremely skilful as well as physically and mentally demanding, work, caring for adult members of their families as well as children. Others who do not have these roles behave in some respects like caged prisoners, unable to liberate their potentialities, subservient to men, often longing for paid employment and less often having the opportunity to fulfil that longing. Through these examples and others, the concepts of employment and unemployment must be enlarged to properly represent people's circumstances and frustrations.

There is also the ambivalent social perception of retirement. Is it, or is it not, to be treated as a form of unemployment? When retirement is compared with unemployment society's attitudes are inconsistent and fundamentally illogical, the stereotype being to bless one and condemn the other, with the mere matter of age accounting for the distinction (Walker A., 'The Social Consequences of Early Retirement', Political Quarterly, Vol. 53, 1982; and Walker A., 'Early Retirement: Release or Refuge from the Labour Market?', the Quarterly Journal of Social Affairs, Vol. 1, No. 3, 1985). There are many thousands of people prematurely retired who are as despairing and unhappy with retirement as others are with unemployment. Too often the conditions, and the sense of ignominy, are the same.

These references help us to perceive the importance of economic institutions not just indirectly causing poverty but directly fostering the social institutions and conventions which create the social rules giving or denying access to employment and hence income. What are these social institutions and conventions? They are conventions like the school leaving age; institutions concerned with apprenticeship — now becoming dominated in British society by the Youth Training Scheme; assumptions that the true place of women is in the home, unpaid; and laws as well as conventions about the fixed age of retirement. We are led inevitably to these issues if we search for the causes of poverty in the nature, extent and development of unemployment and underemployment.

The Causes of Unemployment:
The Thatcher Government's Philosophy

The Thatcher Government is of the opinion that people will only work when they have to. This overarching philosophy colours not only the policy on state benefits but also the theory behind Ministers' understanding of the labour market in general and unemployment in particular. They understand 'going out to work' within a framework of individual choice from a range of different alternatives. From the employer's point of view wages have to be sufficiently low to make it worthwhile to make the offer. From the employee's point of view the wages have to be sufficiently attractive to make the acceptance of the offer worthwhile. These networks of offers and choices make up the Labour Market as an institution.

According to this philosophy unemployment is supposed to be caused by people 'pricing' themselves out of jobs in two ways. First, having accepted the 'offer' of employment at one wage, they will price themselves out of a job when they are in work if they increase the wage demanded to such an extent that the firm they are working for no longer finds it profitable to offer employment at all. Given this lack of profitability the employer will withdraw the offer and take their capital and offers of employment elswhere. Thus when the offers of jobs gets smaller, the labour market diminishes. Second, the unemployed workers can still price themselves out of a job by expecting to be able to obtain a level of remuneration which no putative employer will offer. Having 'priced themselves' out of a job in the first place they are then guilty of 'expecting too much' and therefore remain unemployed. On this reasoning both the construction of unemployment and its maintenance is caused by the expectations of the working person being higher than the offers that the employer is prepared to make.

Such a philosophy has very strong economic and social policy implications. It is not at all a policy of laissez faire but depends on powerful interventions by Government in order to structure both employment and unemployment. In the first instance employees must be encouraged to resist increasing their wages above the level that employers will be able to offer them in employment. This calls for a policy of keeping wages down and discouraging employers from settling negotiations too generously as well as employees and their representatives from making excessive demands. If this succeeds the only way that work will return is if the wages are sufficiently low for employers to bother to provide work. So the low wage policy must remain. But given the philosophical dynamics, it MUST be supplemented by a policy of lowering the expectations of those unemployed, for if they continue to maintain their expectations at the level where they 'priced themselves out of the market' then no new jobs will emerge. So their lives and expectations must be changed.

This, in turn, can be achieved only by making life for the unemployed horrible. Under those circumstances people will decide to lower their expectations and will be prepared to accept work at a lower price to escape such privation and misery. Down will come wages and up will go the number of jobs.

In relation to the London economy there are elements of this philosophy that fail to come to grips with reality. The Government assumes that the initially passive partner in the relationship, the employer, will provide jobs at some stage. But if employers have left the area for reasons that go beyond the level of wages then simply changing that level by lowering potential workers' expectations will not bring them back. There are, of course, in the world of multi-national capital a very great number of complex rationales for closing a factory and moving its production elsewhere. This can involve complex financial and investment strategies together with product market projections and international political and trading assessments. The real world consists of powerful institutional networks with relatively small nerve centres of control. They amount to being structural not personal or individual factors. Even in the case of small firms the rationale for taking on extra employees is primarily constrained not by wages levels but by the size of demand for the product or service (See for example the admitted constraints in the Government's own White paper, 'Burdens on Business', HMSO, London, 1984). Of course this level of demand is itself inhibited by a lack of money in the economy caused in largest measure by high unemployment.

Far too much of the Government's explanation for unemployment depends upon individual choices being made at the same time by a large number of very different people. Unemployed people are assumed to be able to choose work if they want; the responsibility to look for and help create work is theirs. Unemployment therefore is supposed to be an aggregation of individual choices and not a matter of structural changes in the form and nature of the economy. This fundamental, and absurd, mistake lies at the heart of the Government's policies on economic and social deprivation.

Conclusion

Although the percentage officially unemployed in Greater London is a little smaller than average for Britain the city holds the largest concentration of unemployed in the industrialised world, and the real total is at least 150,000 larger than the total of over 400,000 admitted by the Government. The problem has been growing faster in inner city boroughs and wards than in outlying more prosperous areas, and affects young people, blacks and people with disabilities disproportionately. The rate for women is only two thirds that for men but has been catching up since 1979 and the real as distinct from the official rate is at least as high as that for men.

The survey is producing hard evidence of the uncounted unemployed. They include men and women not eligible to claim benefit because a husband or wife is in paid employment or because they have exhausted their entitlement to benefit, men under 65 who are receiving an occupational pension and want paid employment, and men and women of pensionable age who do not wish to be prematurely retired and want part-time or full-time paid employment.

The Government's analysis of the extent and causes of unemployment is found wanting. The catastrophic decline in manufacturing industry in London, taking half-a-million jobs out of the economy in little more than a decade, is due not so much to technological change and uncompetitively high wages as a failure to provide sufficient investment to keep pace with international as well as technological changes, and a failure to plan for the kind of service jobs and labour intensive specialised productive jobs which will be required in the society of the future. That failure is primarily the responsibility of political as well as industrial leadership and management. In London the economy is becoming rapidly more unbalanced, with the huge growth of jobs in banking, finance and insurance partly concealing the savage pruning of London's manufacturing industry. London's economy has become more precarious and more dependent on overseas economies very quickly. The abandonment of controls and slavish adherence to an international market has not merely enlarged unemployment and brought the threat of insecurity to many wage-earners but paradoxically increased the insecurity of the rich as well. In London thousands with very high incomes are serving multi-national conglomerates and powerful and rich international elites rather than national or social needs. Their international masters may not want them for very long.

4.

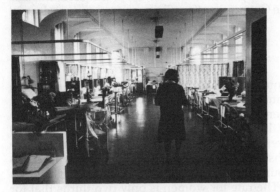

Social Polarisation and Trends in Deaths in the 1980s

Unemployment is a harbinger of other misfortune. There is a widening gap between different areas of London which is demonstrated not only by trends in unemployment but by other forms of material and social deprivation. There are a number of available statistical indicators. They show some areas experiencing a greater concentration of certain problems at the same time as other areas are becoming relieved of them. The pattern is by no means consistent but examples are overcrowding, poor housing facilities, frequent moves of house and lack of assets or income, as measured by non-ownership of a car and by rough measures of cash income. More unequal living standards also correspond with new relationships with the economy. Jobs for women have expanded in some local labour markets and have contracted in others. And although a region like London allows people to travel long distances to work the deterioration of local economic opportunites and social amenities forces people who can afford it to move away from the area and imprisons others in conditions from which there is little or no means of escape. Certain minorities become more prominent in these areas with worsening economic conditions because their incomes and opportunities of getting paid work are low, their dependencies are often restrictive and their need to counter discrimination and not merely maintain cultural practices familiar to them draws them together. They are obliged to resort to places

TABLE 4.1
Trends in Most and Least Deprived Boroughs of Greater London 1971-1981

Characteristic	Real change in rate per 1,000 compared with average change			
	Hackney	Tower Hamlets	Sutton	Bromley
Unemployment	+27	+14	−11	− 8
Work outside borough	+34	+23	−20	−25
Overcrowding	+ 2	+15	− 5	− 8
Lone Parents	+18	− 2	−19	− 1
'New Commonwealth' Residents	+20	+28	−11	−19
Exclusive household amenities	− 1	+28	0	0
Moved within last year (indicator of residential insecurity)	− 8	+10	− 9	−14
Women working	−26	−46	+16	+14

Source: Congdon, P, *Social Structure in the London Boroughs: Evidence from the 1981 Census and Changes Since 1971*, Statistical series No.28, Greater London Council, 1984.

where they can get a home and a modicum of social support at least cost. Some areas therefore become backwaters of the city's economy. While this is not a new process it is becoming very marked in the London of the 1980s.

Table 4.1 illustrates these three trends. It compares the rate of change in the richest and poorest boroughs of London, according to Census information for 1971 and 1981. The changes on these (admittedly limited) indicators are not consistent but it can be seen that in both richest and poorest boroughs there has been a tendency to depart further from average conditions and circumstances. Higher than average growth in unemployment has driven more people to work outside the borough, and the numbers of women working have fallen particularly sharply. In inner London boroughs with large increases in unemployment, such as Hackney, Tower Hamlets and Newham, the number of women in paid employment grew much less than expected in the 1970s. By contrast, in outer London boroughs with small increases in unemployment, like Hillingdon, Sutton and Bromley, the number grew much more than expected. Areas with high rates of unemployment tend also to be areas with below-average numbers of households with two or more wage-earners and with disproportionately large numbers with low earnings. This helps to explain why the trends in unemployment represent a more general polarisation of economic and social conditions.

The number of people in some areas with relatively worsening

TABLE 4.2
Income Distribution in Most and Least Deprived London Boroughs (1984)

Borough	Z Score (7 Variables)	Per cent of households with	
		Less than £6,000 pa	More than £15,000
Most Deprived			
Hackney	9.21	64.8	3.3
Tower Hamlets	8.55	69.6	3.3
Islington	7.04	57.4	10.4
Lambeth	6.87	52.9	9.3
Newham	6.75	55.6	5.0
Least Deprived			
Harrow	−6.66	38.9	15.8
Sutton	−7.74	39.3	15.9
Bexley	−7.96	38.5	9.2
Bromley	−8.17	37.4	16.3
Havering	−8.30	43.7	8.6

Notes

Z score based on following variables:
  i. per cent (of economically active who are unemployed);
  ii. per cent of economically active and retired who are semi-skilled or unskilled;
  iii. per cent of households overcrowded;
  iv. per cent of households lacking exclusive use of two basic amenities;
  v. per cent of households that were single parent households;
  vi. per cent of households headed by someone born in New Commonwealth or Pakistan;
  vii. pensioners in one person households.

Source: Saunders MB. GLTS Household Survey: Borough Translations, GLTS Analysis Report No.6, TS Note No.156, GLC, County Hall Aug 1985 (and Z Scores from GLC Intelligence Unit).

conditions who are black or in one-parent families has also grown. A statistical report prepared for the GLC concluded that there was 'a widening gap between boroughs containing few deprived groups and those containing many' (Congdon P., Social Structure in the London Boroughs: Evidence from the 1981 Census and Changes since 1971, Statistical Series No. 28, Greater London Council, 1984, p.24). During the 1970s there were disproportionately large increases in ethnic minorities living in boroughs like Tower Hamlets, Newham, and Southwark. In Hammersmith and Fulham and Islington the increases were less than expected, partly because of a marked 'gentrification' of housing in the former borough and a marked expansion of new council housing (to which access was sometimes difficult) in the latter. Boroughs with above average numbers of Asians in 1971 (Newham, Tower Hamlets, Brent and Ealing) had numbers even more above average in 1981, while boroughs with below average numbers in 1971 were even further below average ten years later (Bexley, Bromley and Sutton).

When measured features of deprivation are combined together the differences between poor and rich boroughs become striking. Table 4.2 shows the wide gulf which exists between boroughs like Hackney, Tower Hamlets, Islington, Lambeth and Newham, on the one hand, and boroughs like Harrow, Sutton, Bexley, Bromley and Havering on the other. The measure of deprivation adopted by the Intelligence Unit of the GLC (now the London Research Centre) is explained in a note to the table. Table 4.2 also shows the big difference between the two sets of boroughs in the spread of incomes. The correlation between low income and deprivation is marked, on this evidence. Hackney and Tower Hamlets stand out as having high percentages of the population at low levels of income, with very few indeed at high levels of income.

Fall in the Real Incomes of the Poor

The real incomes of the poorest quarter of households in London declined between 1971 and 1981 while the incomes of the richest quarter increased, as measured at the lower and upper quartiles. At the lower quartile there was a decline by 4 per cent and at the upper quartile an increase of as much as 24 per cent. The evidence shows that this polarisation was taking place before the present Government took office, and was more marked in London than in the country as a whole (GLC, Low Incomes in London: Evidence for the Family Expenditure Survey, Reviews and Studies Series, No. 20, Greater London Council, 1983, p.21).

More recent trends in the distribution of incomes are shown in Table 4.3. The table is based on data drawn from the Family Expenditure Survey, an annual survey of incomes and expenditure conducted by the Department of Employment. Because it is a sample survey the results for sub-groups vary marginally from year to year, as would be expected, but the sample is large and nationally representative and the trends which are manifest are internally consistent. The trends are also consistent with evidence from other sources.

There are at least three firm conclusions which emerge from Table 4.3 and associated official data:- (i) the real incomes of the poorest sections of the population of Britain as a whole as well as of Greater London have in fact diminished since 1979; (ii) inequality of income has become much more pronounced in a short span of years, and (iii) such polarisation of experience is more marked in London than in the country as a whole.

The data reproduced in Table 4.3 are for *gross* household income in the years in question. The data for *disposable* household income (that is, income after tax) follow the same pattern. The

TABLE 4.3
Changes in Gross Household Income of Relatively Rich and Poor
at constant (1985) prices (£ per week)

	Greater London			
	Lowest Decile	Lower Quartile	Upper Quartile	Highest Decile
1979	55.04	104.57	305.07	401.29
1981	62.26	106.55	325.87	441.06
1983	62.97	97.35	334.79	463.41
1984	51.22	94.10	335.78	488.32
1985	47.10	96.33	341.82	473.20
Percentage Change 1979-85	−17	−8	+12	+18
	Britain			
1979	54.19	95.09	270.12	372.43
1981	58.72	98.20	285.26	389.12
1983	58.58	92.82	276.49	384.74
1984	50.80	88.86	288.66	402.28
1985	49.00	88.41	296.95	416.76
Percentage Increase 1979-85	−10	−7	+10	+12

Source: Department of Employment, (1980-1986) Annual Reports of the Family Expenditure Survey, London, HMSO.

figures for 1979-85 are set out in Appendix 3 (with the exception of the years before 1983 for Greater London, for which the data are not available). The most important conclusion from the evidence in Table 4.3 and Appendix 3 deserves to be repeated: the real incomes of the poorest sections of the population have diminished since 1979. This applies to the poorest quarter — 14 million people — and not just the poorest tenth. In Britain, at 1985 prices, disposable household income per week of the poorest tenth had fallen between 1979 and 1985 by £5.15 per week, or nearly 10 per cent, and of the poorest quarter by £2.47 per week, or 3 per cent. Disposable incomes at the top end increased substantially: of the richest tenth by £25.16 per week, or 8.5 per cent. This weekly increase of £25.16 represents more than half the disposable weekly income of the poorest tenth and gives a graphic illustration of the extent of redistribution which has taken place in a short span of years. Within poor households some groups have lost more than others. The poorest tenth of pensioners have gained marginally but there has been virtually no change in the purchasing power of the poorest quarter of pensioners, with couples still at the level of their 1979 incomes and single pensioners more than £2 per week worse off. By contrast, poor families with children have had a profound cut in incomes — couples with one child in the poorest tenth losing by £17, with two children by £19 and with three children by £32 per week. This is

TABLE 4.4
Variations in Death Rates for Selected London Boroughs
1979-1982

Death rates as a percentage of Bromley rates:

Age	Bromley	Males Sutton	Hackney	Tower Hamlets
0-1	100	102	157	130
30-34	100	82	149	139
40-44	100	87	189	217
50-54	100	113	187	220
60-64	100	100	141	160
70-74	100	105	117	127
80-84	100	98	107	118
Females				
0-1	100	134	138	184
30-34	100	79	88	119
40-44	100	110	178	132
50-54	100	84	136	142
60-64	100	113	140	145
70-74	100	105	113	127
80-84	100	98	111	104

Source: Calculated from Hills C. and Hollis J. (1986) *Greater London Life Tables 1979-82*, Statistical Series No.50, GLC.

partly a reflection of rising unemployment, but also cuts in benefit, rises in taxes and depreciation of wages.

Deprivation and Mortality in London

There is also a high correlation between deprivation and mortality. This can be shown for large and for small areas. We can begin with the 33 boroughs. There is a big difference in expectation of life according to borough of residence. For example, the expectation of life of males at birth in Bromley and Sutton is about four years longer than it is in Hackney and Tower Hamlets. For females the difference is about three years (Hills C., and Hollis J., Greater London Lifetables: 1979-82. Statistical Series No. 50, Greater London Council, 1986, p.7). The accompanying map shows the boroughs where the expectation of life is relatively low. These include Hammersmith and Fulham, Islington, Hackney, Tower Hamlets, Newham, Barking and Dagenham and Lambeth. In 1984 Harrow was the London borough with the lowest SMR (82) and Tower Hamlets the highest (114, or 39 per cent higher) (Annual Abstract of Greater London Statistics, 1984-85, 1986, Greater London Council, 1986, p.33). The differences in mortality tend to be largest in middle life and least in childhood (with the exception of the first year of life)

MAP 4.1

Life Expectancy at Birth of Males and Females, Greater London, 1979-1982

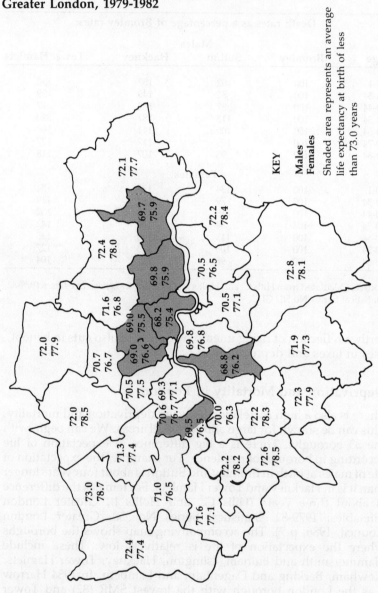

KEY

Males
Females

Shaded area represents an average life expectancy at birth of less than 73.0 years

TABLE 4.5
Expectation of life in Most and Least Deprived Boroughs of Greater London
1979-1982

Borough	Z. Score (7 Variables)	Expectation of life	
Most Deprived		Males	Females
Hackney	9.21	69.02	75.53
Tower Hamlets	8.55	68.18	75.42
Islington	7.04	69.11	76.64
Lambeth	6.87	68.75	76.24
Newham	6.75	69.78	75.87
Least Deprived			
Harrow	−6.66	73.03	78.67
Sutton	−7.74	72.25	77.93
Bexley	−7.96	72.16	78.36
Bromley	−8.17	72.75	78.08
Havering	−8.30	72.08	77.68

Note: Z. Scores calculated on variables listed in Note to Table 4.2.
Source: Hills C. and Hollis J. Greater London Life tables, 1979-82, GLC Statistical Series No.50, Greater London Council 1986.

and early adulthood. The death rates of males aged 40-44 and 50-54 in Tower Hamlets and Hackney were around twice those in boroughs like Bromley. The ratio falls but is still significant among old people. Table 4.4 compares the relative death rates of four London boroughs for a period of three years, 1979-1982.

The differences in expectation of life between boroughs correlate highly with combined as well as specific measures of deprivation. Thus, when the boroughs are ranked on the combined indicator of deprivation used by the Intelligence Unit of the GLC those ranked highest are found to have the lowest average expected years of life, and vice-versa. Details are given in Table 4.5. Every borough is also plotted in Figure 4.1, showing average life expectancy in relation to score on the overall index of deprivation used by the GLC Intelligence Unit. These illustrations help to convey the high correlation between deprivation and ill-health or death, as measured by life expectancy.

Some people may be surprised that the differences are not larger than as given in the illustrations. Two things should be remembered. One is the comparatively large size of these London boroughs. Excepting the City of London they range in population from 130,000 to 320,000 and include widely different communities within their boundaries, some with relatively good and others with relatively bad health. The other thing to remember is that the figures are based on current mortality experience. The number of expected years of life is an estimate based on the extrapolation of present

FIGURE 4.1: Average (M+F) Life Expectancy 1979-82 plotted against Index of Deprivation (1981) for London Boroughs

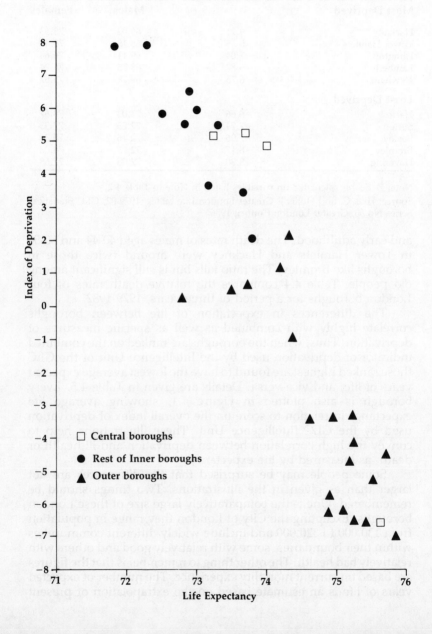

Index of Deprivation (y-axis)

Life Expectancy (x-axis)

□ Central boroughs
● Rest of Inner boroughs
▲ Outer boroughs

mortality rates into the future and not a representation of the experience of people dying in recent years.

Deprivation and Death in 755 wards

The geography of death has been mapped in a number of reports on different regions of Britain in recent years but remains to be fully exploited in the analysis of small areas. Some possibilities can be illustrated for wards. London has 755 wards. Many of these are by no stretch of the imagination 'natural' communities but many are, in the sense that their boundaries contain substantial homogeneous groups linked by economic and social relationships as well as by location. More knowledge of their characteristics will help us to understand much better the causes as well as the nature of contemporary economic and social problems. There are important analyses by ward of multiple deprivation using Census indicators (Davies H., 1981 Census — A Ward Index of Deprivation, Statistical Series No. 35, Greater London Council, 1984; and Armstrong B., 1981 Census : Ward and Borough Indices for Greater London, Statistical Series No. 30, Greater London Council, 1984). However, there are other data of an administrative kind which are available to education and other departments of local councils which could be correlated and used to deepen the analysis, and in particular there are mortality and other health data which could be related to sophisticated indices of multiple deprivation (as they have been in some regions, for example, the north of England and South Yorkshire). The key to better understanding of present patterns of multiple deprivation lies as much in the patient re-assembly of existing stocks of data, as in new and costly forms of research. This is the key also to more effective policy.

As a basis for the new survey research in London all 755 wards in London were ranked according to their level of material deprivation. After examining a number of possibilities the best available summary measure seemed to be to combine four criteria or indices: per cent of economically active persons who are unemployed; per cent of households found to be overcrowded; per cent of households not owning their own home; and per cent of households lacking a car. Needless to add, these are not ideal indicators for the purpose of studying multiple deprivation in London. They are the best available from the Census of 1981. This is explained in Appendix 1. Since much of the research is designed to explore the nature of deprivation and poverty a background account of the meaning and optional operational applications of these two concepts, as well as the criteria of deprivation pursued in our interviews, will be found in Appendix 1 in this interim report.

The differences found among the 755 wards are very wide. This can be seen by comparing the most deprived with the least deprived wards. Table 4.6 illustrates the contrast for the 10 wards at top and

TABLE 4.6
London Wards Ranked High and Low on Measure of Multiple Deprivation (1981)

Ranked Ward	Borough	Z score index	Per Cent			
			Unemployed	Over-crowded	Not owning home	Not owning car
1 Spitalfields	Tower Hamlets	8.4	21.9	28.3	96.5	79.6
2 St Mary's	Tower Hamlets	6.9	19.5	16.5	95.2	74.0
3 Carlton	Brent	6.5	21.7	10.3	97.6	77.0
4 Golborne	Kensington & Chelsea	6.3	19.1	13.2	93.1	73.7
5 Shadwell	Tower Hamlets	6.3	17.3	14.1	98.1	71.3
6 Blackwall	Tower Hamlets	6.1	21.1	11.4	97.5	68.7
7 Haggerston	Hackney	6.1	18.0	13.2	97.3	72.1
8 St Katherine's	Tower Hamlets	6.1	15.4	15.7	97.1	69.0
9 White City	Hammersmith & Fulham	6.0	17.6	12.4	88.7	74.3
10 Kings Park	Hackney	5.9	19.3	11.5	97.8	68.1
746 Falconwood	Bexley	−8.8	3.2	2.1	2.4	25.4
747 Emerson Park	Havering	−8.8	4.3	1.3	6.0	16.3
748 Crofton	Bromley	−8.9	2.6	1.1	9.8	18.2
749 West Wickham North	Bromley	−9.1	3.1	0.6	10.0	18.5
750 Farnborough	Bromley	−9.4	3.2	1.1	7.8	15.0
751 Biggin Hill	Bromley	−10.0	3.1	2.0	9.9	7.9
752 Woodcote	Sutton	−10.0	4.8	0.7	14.5	6.6
753 Cheam South	Sutton	−10.7	2.8	0.6	8.9	11.0
754 Selsdon	Croydon	−10.8	2.6	0.5	6.7	13.5
755 Cranham West	Havering	−11.0	3.2	0.9	4.1	12.4

Source: Produced with the help of the London Research Centre (formerly GLC, now the London Residuary Body).

FIGURE 4.2: Ranking of GLC Wards on an Index of Multiple Deprivation Calculated from Four Indicators

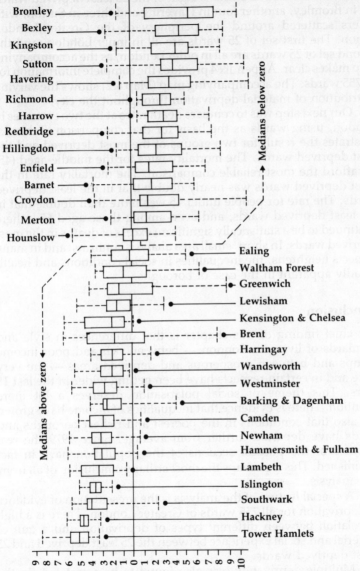

Note: The 'spread' of each quarter of the wards in each borough are shown either by dashed lines or rectangles.

bottom of the scale. On every criterion they are quite distinct, as the overall scores of variation also make clear. Another method of demonstrating the distinctiveness of wards in different London boroughs is illustrated in Figure 4.2. The location of relatively deprived and non-deprived wards in London is also of considerable interest. Seven of the 25 most deprived wards are in Tower Hamlets, and another five in Hackney. Three are in Brent and three also in Lambeth. At the other extreme eight of the 25 least deprived wards are in Bromley, another four in Havering and three in Sutton, with others scattered around the periphery of the Greater London region. The first set of 25 wards are all in inner London, and the second set of 25 wards are all in outer London, as the accompanying map makes clear. Appendix 4 provides the complete information for all 755 wards. The accompanying map (Map 4.2) shows the varying distribution of material deprivation throughout the city.

Our next step was to compare death rates at the two extremes in London, using wards as the basis for that comparison. Table 4.7 illustrates the result for two groups of the most deprived and the least deprived wards. The mortality rates for the middle-aged (45-64) afford the most reliable comparison. The mortality rate in the most deprived wards was nearly double that in the least deprived wards. The rate for people under 45 was more than double that in the least deprived wards, and even among those aged 65+ there continued to be a statistically significant excess of deaths in the most deprived wards. In short, small area analysis confirms, and in many respects heightens, the inequalities in social conditions and health broadly apparent in the case of boroughs.

Conclusion

The chief finding of this chapter is that differences in style and standards of living in London — between rich and poor income groups and between prosperous and deprived areas — are very wide and in certain respects have been getting wider in the last 15 years. This theme of social polarisation deserves a lot more attention. There is evidence that inequalities of income have grown but also that conditions in the poorest and richest boroughs and wards have departed further from average. Since 1979 the real incomes of the poorest sections of the population have in fact diminished. This is perhaps the most striking conclusion of all from this analysis.

A special feature of the analysis is the presentation of evidence of deprivation for all 755 wards of Greater London. There is a high correlation between different types of deprivation and a gulf of material and social experience between the 25 least deprived and 25 most deprived wards.

Multiple deprivation was also found to be correlated for the principal age-groups with relatively high mortality. Below the pensionable ages mortality was about twice as high in the 25 most deprived wards as in the 25 least deprived wards and was still significantly higher for those of pensionable age.

MAP 4.2
Wards Ranked on Multiple Deprivation Indicator

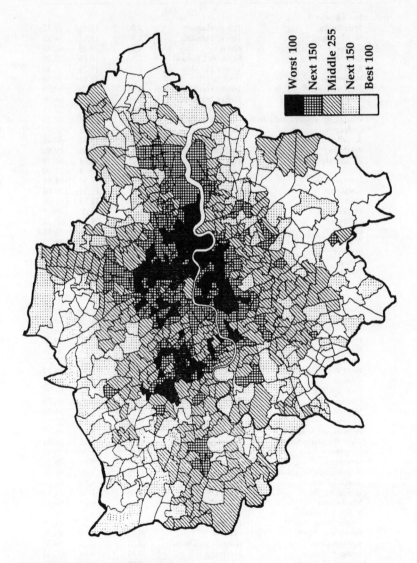

Source: 1981 Census of Population

Produced by the London Research Centre

TABLE 4.7
Mortality Rates 1982-84 in 25 Most Deprived and 25 Least Deprived London Wards

Ward	Borough	Under 45	45-64	65+
		Crude Mortality rates per 1,000 population		
Most Deprived				
Spitalfields	Tower Hamlets	0.90	14.16	75.41
St. Mary's	Tower Hamlets	1.57	18.92	54.55
Carlton	Brent	1.13	9.80	67.42
Golborne	Kens. & Chelsea	1.66	10.75	73.97
Shadwell	Tower Hamlets	1.70	14.23	77.40
Haggerston	Hackney	0.95	10.85	48.86
Blackwall	Tower Hamlets	0.94	10.75	59.68
St. Katherine's	Tower Hamlets	1.68	13.81	66.96
Kings Park	Hackney	0.94	15.28	72.19
White City & Shepherds Bush	H'Smith & Fulham	1.40	13.18	67.13
Ordnance	Newham	1.49	14.84	67.99
Angell	Lambeth	1.83	13.37	67.48
Westdown	Hackney	1.03	10.56	69.92
St. Dunstan's	Tower Hamlets	1.28	11.54	64.28
Liddle	Southwark	1.06	10.19	71.30
Harrow Road	Westminster	1.07	9.34	61.14
Eastdown	Hackney	1.07	11.50	48.04
Queen's Park	Westminster	1.67	11.35	61.39
Stonebridge	Brent	1.36	8.00	48.01
Larkhall	Lambeth	1.05	9.57	68.12
Rectory	Hackney	0.85	6.89	46.14
Avondale	Kens. & Chelsea	1.19	9.52	48.29
Weavers	Tower Hamlets	1.37	11.81	59.42
Vassall	Lambeth	1.15	10.45	93.39
Westbourne	Westminster	1.40	10.50	78.54
Mean of 25 Wards		1.27	11.59	63.78
Least Deprived				
Cranham Heath	Havering	0.35	7.02	55.91
Selsdon	Croydon	0.73	6.86	53.62
Cheam South	Sutton	0.43	6.21	106.02
Woodcote	Sutton	1.07	7.87	40.72
Biggin Hill	Bromley	0.61	8.06	50.34
Farnborough	Bromley	1.14	6.04	57.75
West Wickham North	Bromley	0.66	4.74	45.24
Crofton	Bromley	0.78	7.77	46.92
Emerson Park	Havering	0.62	5.48	54.58
Falconwood	Bexley	0.74	6.30	50.75
Malden Manor	Kingston u Thames	0.00	6.03	54.35
Ickenham	Hillingdon	0.85	7.14	52.69
Petts Wood & Knoll	Bromley	0.48	6.10	46.13
West Wickham South	Bromley	0.70	5.95	46.84
Upminster	Havering	0.52	7.00	50.92
Shortlands	Bromley	0.74	5.90	48.29
Woodcote & Couldson W.	Croydon	0.75	9.07	92.80
North Cheam	Sutton	0.15	6.92	46.51
Worcester Pk. S.	Sutton	0.38	7.38	41.10
Monkhams	Redbridge	0.64	6.09	52.45
B'don & Penhill	Bexley	0.48	5.87	49.91
Pinner West	Harrow	0.35	6.30	42.60
Headstone North	Harrow	0.72	5.55	46.20
Tolworth East	Kingston u Thames	0.40	7.12	48.70
Ardleigh Green	Havering	0.81	4.84	47.44
Mean of 25 Wards		**0.62**	**6.56**	**55.52**

Source: London Research Centre.

Note: These are not age-standardised rates.

5.

The Growth of Poverty and the Inadequacy of Benefits

What are we finding? The data from thousands of interviews carried out between the autumn of 1985 to the autumn of 1986 are still being edited and analysed but it is possible at this early date to convey features of the evidence as well as individual illustrations. Other sources of information about incomes and living standards will also be reviewed. A discussion of the meaning of poverty will be found in Appendix 2 — as distinguished from the meaning of deprivation (Appendix 1).

Earnings in Greater London are larger than elsewhere but poverty seems to be nearly as extensive and in certain respects more severe. According to the Government's New Earnings Survey, full-time earnings of men in 1984 averaged £215 per week, compared with £179 in Britain as a whole. The corresponding earnings of women averaged £143 and £117 respectively. Fewer men and women also earned low wages. Thus, only 13 per cent of men working full-time earned less than £120 per week, compared with 22 per cent in the country as a whole. Only 20 per cent of women working full-time earned less than £100 per week in Greater London, compared with as many as 43 per cent in Britain. The differences are pronounced for other earners — for part-time and occasional employees and, within the average figures for all types of

TABLE 5.1
Distribution of Income: London and Britain (1985)

Quantiles	Aggregate gross household income (£ per week)		Aggregate disposable household income (£ per week)	
	Greater London	Britain	Greater London	Britain
Lowest decile	47.1	49.0	46.6	48.4
Lower quartile	96.3	88.4	89.5	83.4
Median	207.5	184.7	167.5	152.7
Upper quartile	341.8	296.9	261.5	232.7
Highest decile	473.2	416.8	367.8	322.6

Source: Department of Employment, *Family Expenditure Survey 1985*, HMSO, London, pp.68-69.

workers, for non-manual and manual workers. (For all the detailed information see the Annual Abstract of Greater London Statistics, 1984-85, GLC, London, 1986, pp.72-73).

However, millions in the London population are not in paid employment at all. They depend on incomes which are not higher, or very little higher, than those of people living elsewhere in the country. These incomes consist mainly of social security benefits. There is also a very different structure of costs in London, which is recognised by many employers in the form of a 'London allowance' which accounts in part for the higher earnings reported. Costs like housing, transport and certain foodstuffs, are higher. This means that the apparent advantage of that part of the city's population in paid employment is not so pronounced as the statistics on earnings suggest. But it also means that those living on standard social security benefits are at a disadvantage.

The spread of gross and disposable incomes is shown in Table 5.1. It can be seen that at the lower levels, despite higher costs in the metropolis, incomes exceed those for Britain as a whole only by a small amount. What stands out is the substantially higher real incomes of the most prosperous 25 per cent. Compared with the population in general, there are far more rich and prosperous people in Greater London. The spread of inequality is wider there than in Britain.

Because there are almost as many people in London as elsewhere who are unemployed, retired or otherwise not in paid employment and living on standard social security benefits, the capital has almost the same proportion as the rest of the country living in poverty or on the lowest incomes. Indeed, one of the objects of the London research survey is to check and explore the approximate estimates of poverty given in Table 5.2 from official sources. Conservative assumptions have been applied to the

TABLE 5.2
Numbers in Poverty: London and Britain (1983)

Income in relation to supplementary benefit standard	Greater London (000s)	Britain (000s)
Below SB standard	300 ⎫	2,700 ⎫
Receiving SB	600 ⎬ 1,800	6,130 ⎬ 16,380
At or up to 40 per cent above SB standard	900 ⎭	7,550 ⎭
Other levels of income	4,620	37,325
Total	6,420	53,705

Note: Figures for London have been estimated on the basis of Government information available for Britain as a whole.

Source: DHSS special analysis for Britain, placed in House of Commons library on 27 July 1986.

national figures on incomes relative to the supplementary benefit standard to produce estimates for London. The make-up of the population by age in London is not very different from that of Britain, with the same percentage aged 65 and over and very slightly fewer children under 15. Slightly fewer people in London than generally in Britain are unemployed, and there are fewer large families. On the other hand, there are more lone parents, and more people live alone.

Working from Government statistics for Britain, it can be estimated that 1.8 millions in London live in poverty or on the margins of poverty. Of these, at least 300,000 have less income than the current basic rates of supplementary benefit, and another 600,000 actually depend on supplementary benefit (See Table 5.2). These numbers have approximately doubled since the early 1960s. The Government's own statistics for Britain show that the trends have been upwards. Thus, between 1960 and 1983 the number of people with incomes below or on the margins of the supplementary benefit or what was previously called the national assistance standard more than doubled, from 7.4 to 16.4 millions. A large part of this increase occurred between 1979 and 1983. It should be emphasised that the figure of 1.8 millions given above applies not to the present day but to 1983. Although evidence is available for 1984, 1985 and even perhaps 1986 the Government has not published more recent figures than those for 1983.

The numbers have certainly increased since then. For example, dependency has substantially increased. Unemployment has continued to grow, as has the number of people prematurely retired, as well as the number of people aged 75 and over. In London the trend towards smaller households and more people living alone has continued, and there have been substantial increases in certain deprived groups, like the number of households accepted as being homeless. And simultaneous with an increase in the numbers of people being made dependent on low levels of social security those incomes have diminished in real or at least relative terms.

More than 20 steps have been taken by the Government since 1979 to reduce the cost of social security. In aggregate the total has been cut by some £12 billions. Perhaps the most significant cut was the substitution of a price index for an earnings index in the uprating of pensions, and the termination of earnings-related benefits for sickness and unemployment. These three measures alone have reduced the incomes of about 10½ million people from what they would have been by 1987 by an average of over £4 per person per week. The Social Security Act 1986 follows the same strategy as the previous measures of squeezing the poor to make savings in public expenditure, pave the way for further tax cuts, and make even the lowest wages look attractive. The authors of the Technical Annex to the White Paper on the Social Security Bill admitted that 3.8 million people will lose income as a consequence of the introduction of the provisions of the Social Security Act in 1987 and 1988.

The Distribution of Income and the Government's Strategy

An example of the Government's growing insensitivity towards issues of poverty was its indifference towards the need of many elderly and disabled people for additional heating during the desperately severe winter of 1985-86. Interviewers in the present survey were then hard at work. At that time the charge that could be made against Ministers was not simply one of Scrooge-like behaviour in failing to act quickly enough to advise officials of the humane precautionary steps against hypothermia and suffering that might have been taken within their existing powers. It was in seeking to remove those very powers from the discretionary action of future Governments. The Supplementary Benefit (Miscellaneous Amendment) Regulations 1986 actually restrict the right of claimants, including disabled and elderly people, to obtain certain items, like eiderdowns, quilts and hot water bottles, which could formerly have been designated, in emergency situations, as essential. In conditions calling for immediate action they failed to propose any improvement to the universally criticised methods of helping the very young and very old with fuel costs during severe weather. Research by the Policy Studies Institute has shown that 90 per cent of pensioners eligible for help during exceptionally cold weather do not receive it because they do not know of their entitlement. A small recent survey from the Family Policy Studies Centre showed that bedroom temperatures in a council block in Croydon ranged between 43F and 48F. At the same time the temperature at DHSS headquarters at the Elephant and Castle,

South London, was 70F, the standard room temperature which used to be recommended by the DHSS for old people (The Guardian, 3 March, 1986).

Another revealing example was that involving people with disabilities. In February 1986 the Secretary of State for Social Services, Norman Fowler, had the unwanted distinction of provoking the emphatic and implacable hostility of all the major organisations representing disability. They claimed that the Social Security Bill was a cruel deception and far from helping people with disability it did very little for the two-thirds of the disabled population who were in poverty or on the margins of poverty, betrayed the promise in the Conservative Manifesto seven years ago to introduce a 'coherent' income scheme for people with disabilities, and would actually reduce the incomes of thousands of the most severely disabled people in the country — something which no Cabinet Minister in British Parliamentary history had ever contemplated doing. (Letter from six disability organisations: the British Council of Organisations of Disabled People, Disablement Income Group, Disability Alliance, Royal Association for Disability and Rehabilitation, Royal National Institute for the Blind and the Spastics Society, Feb.21, 1986). After promising to consider their representations the Secretary of State did not even deign to write to them in the ensuing months before the Social Security Bill became law.

It is of course not just unemployed or non-employed people who live on low incomes. Earnings at the bottom are being squeezed too. The Government's New Earnings Survey shows widening inequality of earnings. Relative to median earnings top earnings increased in the early and mid 1980s, and bottom earnings decreased. When taken in conjunction with tax concessions and the continuing augmentation of resources and power on the part of managerial, professional and senior administrative groups there has been a very pronounced shift in the distribution of material resources in the last ten and especially seven years. A Government reply in Hansard to a Parliamentary Question provides one precise illustration. There were the following changes per week between 1979 and April 1985 in the take-home pay of people at different levels of pay after income tax and national insurance contributions had been deducted and inflation allowed for:

Changes in Real Take-Home Pay, 1979-1985

Bottom fifth	−£2.33	or	−2.9 per cent
Middle earners	+£2.61		+2.3 per cent
Top fifth	+£20.41		+11.6 per cent

(Hansard, 17 July 1986)

If employer fringe benefits, shifts in housing subsidies and the treatment of personal wealth were taken into the reckoning the difference between top and bottom earners would have been larger. An example of changes taking place throughout Britain is provided by a 1985 report by the Low Pay Unit. The Unit found that approximately 40 per cent of farm workers are now earning less than the supplementary benefit standard. About the same proportion are below the 'decency threshold' set by the Council of Europe's social charter, of which Britain is a signatory.

Severity of Poverty

These are just contemporary instances of the structured analysis required to map the extent of poverty in our society and indicate the forces which are contributing to that situation. Our survey evidence from London includes different representative examples of that poverty — long-term unemployed, low paid, elderly and disabled people and their families and one parent families. Two features must be emphasised. One is that the severity of some people's plight is greater than found in comparable studies 10 or 20 years ago (for example, Townsend P., Poverty in the United Kingdom, Penguin Books, Harmondsworth, 1979, especially Chapter 8). Another way of putting it is that the 'tail' of the distribution of poverty is getting longer. There are instances of people living far below the poverty line. Examples are unemployed people not getting benefit, or who are experiencing long and unnecessary delays in getting giro payments, single unemployed people confused and harrassed by Special Controls teams acting on behalf of the DHSS, homeless people, especially the larger numbers of whom are sleeping rough, and recent (officially approved) immigrant families, like a Bangladeshi family of seven, including five children, interviewed in our survey, who were entitled to, but who were not receiving, supplementary benefit.

There is evidence that the system itself has become less lenient and in many places has gone sour — compared, say, with the National Assistance Board in the 1960s. Here is one authoritative and carefully worded statement:

> 'The experience of poverty is not however simply a matter of how much money is made available. It is also about how it is made available. The way the social security system operates in the Urban Priority Areas was criticised by a number of those who gave evidence to us. The staff in benefit offices are facing increased workloads: they are overworked and overstretched ...Waiting times are long. An efficient system of appointments is difficult to operate. The offices themselves are often drab and demoralising...Any system of social security is bound to have its complexities: adequate resources for the efficient and humane distribution of (and advice about) benefits are therefore needed if the dignity of recipients is to be respected'

(Archbishop of Canterbury's Commission on Urban Priority Areas, Faith in the City: A Call for Action by Church and Nation, Church House Publishing, London, 1985).

During the interviewing in London the problems at one social security office in Westminster were reported:

'The office handles more than 400 claims a day but only admits 50 claimants at any one time after a stabbing incident last year...Many start queuing at 6.45 a.m. to ensure that they will be let in at 9.30 a.m. and receive their benefit before lunch. Those arriving after 11.0 a.m. are not admitted... The office walls have been sprayed with anti-graffiti paint. Eight security guards — outnumbering the counter staff paying benefit — are available if there is trouble...Claimants are not allowed to leave the office until they have been paid, even to get a cup of tea. The office has its own toilet facilities — put in after a cubicle was used as a lavatory — but they are smelly and broken and covered in graffiti. Young people also complained about the treatment they receive from some staff. Some said they had been told to pawn personal jewellery, such as chains, when they asked for extra help for clothes.' (The Guardian, March 14, 1986).

Another press report told of a near riot at the Camberwell office, the petrol bombing of the Greenwich office and two fires in the Battersea office. 'The increasing strain of working in London social security offices is leading to a wave of strikes — and the poor will suffer.' (Laurance, J., 'DHSS Clerks turn Anti-social,' New Society, 21 November, 1986). The effects of current procedures and reduced staffing on groups for whom there is a lot of public sympathy, like the elderly, have also been bad. They have less confidence in the system than formerly and seem less prepared to seek supplementation.

The survey interviewers learned of the experiences and views of claimants. They also met some of the staff who worked in social security offices. For example, one civil servant was on the counter and told us how it felt. 'Working in a pressurised environment, dealing with people who are sometimes at the end of their tether, and you can only deal with the surface problem and there's so much else that is wrong. It upsets me a great deal. I can't switch off from it. I feel nothing's being done. We're very badly under-staffed and I don't think those conditions are necessary.' He wants to leave. He spoke with great feeling about poverty. 'It strikes at all levels... It exists not only financially but through every level of existence.'

The evidence suggests that the service to supplementary benefit claimants in London is far worse than average in Britain and that many claimants experience delays, or interruptions to payments, and more claimants than elsewhere may be deterred from pressing claims for additions or adjustments in their benefits, or may even not claim at all. So the experience of some people in London is both that the cost of living is higher on the same income and that the quality of living is poorer in key respects than in Britain generally.

This theme, of the qualitative and not just material deterioration of conditions experienced by considerable numbers of Londoners, deserves careful attention from social scientists, administrators and politicians. The survey team is also finding a lot more evidence of hostile and fearful relationships within local communities than did a corresponding team 17 years ago. The volume of concern about safety on the streets, burglaries and muggings has gained a major grip nationally and affects ordinary life deeply in an increasing number of communities. Thus, the number of notifiable offences against the person jumped from 47,000 in 1971 to 111,000 in 1983 in England and Wales. The number of burglaries has nearly doubled and the number of robberies has more than tripled during the same period (Central Statistical Office, *Social Trends*, 1985, p.171).

In London the number of notifiable offences known to the police increased from 567,000 in 1980 to 687,000 in 1984. Among the latter were 18,626 cases of violence against the person, 13,532 of robbery, 164,405 of burglary and 365,978 of theft and handling stolen goods (Annual Abstract of Greater London Statistics, 1984-85, GLC, London, 1986, Tables 161-162). Allowing for all the reservations which might be entered about notification and the administration of police statistics, as well as changes in the law, the trend is remorselessly upwards. This makes poverty worse because it isolates people and stultifies community support and the readiness of others to offer comfort and tangible gifts and services to mitigate or compensate for the privations which old people and unemployed people experience. As it becomes more and more extensive poverty multiplies material and also social forms of deprivation.

Inadequacy of Benefit

The second notable feature about our 1986 survey evidence from London is that it demonstrates the inadequacy of existing levels of benefit. That inadequacy deserves to attract more attention than it did during discussions in Parliament leading up to the Social Security Act of 1986. In 1942 Beveridge adopted the 'subsistence' standard of benefit in making recommendations about the level of benefit. This was a predominantly physical standard, which had been first developed at the turn of the century, and those who sponsored it acknowledged the need for income to buy food, shelter and clothing but not to meet the full social obligations and responsibilities of citizenship, parenthood, family membership, friendship, employment and community membership. There is need for theoretical clarification of the differences between these two alternatives and for a full political debate.

In its Green Paper on the Reform of Social Security, published in June 1985, the Government rejected the Beveridge standard and said it had been superseded (Vol. 3, p.5). It went on to suggest that it had been replaced by 'the notion of a relative minimum, with all groups in society having a share in the long-run increase in national prosperity' (Vol. 3, p.16). But the Government did not collect, or review, any evidence about the problems of people living on low incomes nor did it attempt to justify recommended levels of benefit in any reasoned way. As for sharing in national prosperity, it removed this guarantee in 1979 from the poorest people in the country by abolishing the upratings formula for pensions and other benefits, which had been tied to earnings, and substituted a formula related only to changes in prices.

Of the two standards the social or participation standard is scientifically as well as morally preferable. This is mainly on the grounds that needs, including physical needs, are ultimately impossible to define and measure independent of social production, consumption, organisation and custom. That argument has begun to fill the pages of the social science journals and research studies (See for example, Desai M., and Shah A., 'An Econometric Approach to the Measurement of Poverty', Welfare State Programme No. 2, Suntory Toyota International Centre for Economics and Related Disciplines, London School of Economics, 1985; Desai M., 'On Defining the Poverty Threshold', in Golding P., ed., Excluding the Poor, London, Child Poverty Action Group, May 1986; the exchange in the December 1985 issue of Oxford Economic Papers between Sen and Townsend about a sociological approach to a definition of poverty and the papers in the April 1987 issue of the Journal of Social Policy).

There are also a number of overseas social scientists and historians who have begun to develop the case for a revised scientific definition of the income needs of human beings. (They include Aronson N., 'The Making of the US Bureau of Labor Statistics Family Budget Series: Relativism and the Rhetoric of Subsistence', Northwestern University, Evanston, Illinois, Department of Sociology, 1984; Leibfried S., and Tennstedt F., eds., Regulating Poverty and the Splitting of the German Welfare State, Suhrkamp, Frankfurt/Main 1985; and Whiteford P., A Family's Needs: Equivalence Scales, Poverty and Social Security, Research Paper No. 27, Development Division, Department of Social Security, Melbourne, Australia, April 1985).

Britain's meagre standard of benefit has in fact been outstripped in the post-war years by a large number of other countries. As we have seen, the Government argued against the subsistence standard in its 1985 Green Paper but put nothing in its place. Essentially the Government has been arguing against maintaining any kind of national minimum standard of income. This denial does of course have a theoretical basis in monetarism and neo-monetarism, as it does in most of the alternative policy scenarios favouring negative income tax schemes rather than the existing system of social security. What we believe to be important is the evidence we are collecting of the difficulty, if not impossibility for families of living on today's benefits. Moreover, the majority of the public themselves recognise this difference between expectation and reality. We are inviting those interviewed in London to specify what goods and conditions they consider to be 'necessary' in today's conditions. We are also inviting them to estimate what income they consider would represent a poverty line income for a family of their type and size. In both respects public attitudes are far in advance of Government management.

These points can be substantiated from the interviews with those living on different types of benefit — especially for long periods. In view of the importance of having first-hand information we will give examples at some length. For example, a couple aged 30 and 28, with two children aged 6 and 4 were living in a £32 per week council flat in East London. Housing benefit administered by the local authority covered the rent, and the family also received £55 per week supplementary benefit plus £14 child benefit for the two children. Their income of £69 per week was marginally above the scale rates of supplementary benefit prevailing at the time (£47.85 for a couple plus £10.10 for each child under 11 years, adding to an entitlement of £68.05). The mother estimated that the income needed by the family to avoid poverty was £160 and the father (in an independent interview) £170 per week. They had no other form of income and no assets. They possessed only five of the 21 consumer durables about which questions are asked in the course of the interviews. Thus, they had no telephone, iron, freezer or carpet. There were 9 durables which they considered necessary but which they said they could not afford. There were a further six items in a list of housing facilities which they considered necessary to a family and which also they could not afford. There was little space indoors and nowhere outdoors where young children could play safely. They moved house three times in the previous 5 years and had been in their present home only 3 months. Although there was a central heating system it was not used, and was not on during any of the interviewer's calls during that winter. It was a substandard council flat, with damp, broken floorboards and bad decoration.

The mother said she was in poor health, was not eating enough, had too little money, not enough sleep, and was worried about the family's flat and surroundings and generally about the future. She had gone without several meals in the last fortnight to meet the needs of her family (Interestingly, her husband said he had not missed any meals in that period). There were three days when 'the money ran out . We only had bread and butter and a couple of tins of soup — all we could afford — all that was in the house, plus what the older one got at school.' On several of the dietary indicators the family were deprived. 'We don't have the right diet. We have mucky, greasy stuff all the time. It is all we can afford. I would like us to have more fresh food, fruit and meat, but can't afford it.' The same point kept re-surfacing. When asked to define poverty she said, 'Going without things. You can't feed or clothe your kids or take them out. Eating bad food because that's all you can afford.' No one in the family had had a holiday in 1985. She gave detailed information about her family duties. They added up to a total of 72 hours a week, 24 hours of which were services strictly concerned with child care and the rest forms of housework. Nonetheless, she said she had wanted to get a paid job for the last four years and had made efforts recently to find employment like her former job (up to the age of 21) as a waitress in a cafe.

The husband had been a roadsweeper with a gross wage of £70 per week until two years previously. He had been unemployed all that time. He is epileptic and also suffers from chest trouble, which restricts his mobility. He seemed depressed and showed up strongly on various indicators of subjective deprivation. He was preoccupied with the effects of too little money, unemployment, bad housing, heavy traffic and air pollution on his health and felt he had no one to whom he could tell his troubles. The unattainability of a 'decent' wage vied with ill-health as a reason in his own mind for his continued unemployment. During extensive efforts to find employment 'I have been offered work below £2 per hour but that would be less than I'm getting on the dole....I would consider any kind of work but I need a decent wage.' His unpaid work in the home amounted in total to only 3 hours a week. 'You cant give your kids what you want to give them — good clothes and good food — that's poverty.' Both husband and wife did not categorise themselves as working-class but as 'poor' and they consistently ranked themselves as worse off than family, neighbours, and the average in Britain. They said they had been in poverty all their lives.

It is not easy on such evidence to argue that the supplementary benefit scale rates confer an 'adequate' income. And such cases are not exceptional (the data tapes will be available for public access from the autumn of 1987). A former carpenter in his 40s, living with his wife and two teenage children in Newham had an income of £70 supplementary benefit and £7 child benefit. Rent of £32 per week for his council flat was met from housing benefit administered by the council. He had been unemployed for nearly 14 months. The telephone had been cut off and the family owed £500 in unpaid gas bills. Neither he and his wife nor the children had had a holiday away from home in 1985. They think that a cooked breakfast and two hot meals a day are necessary for a family of their type but cannot afford them. They itemised clothing, bedlinen, furniture and household repairs which were urgently needed but could not be provided. He suffers badly now from bronchial asthma, as does his daughter, and during the harsh winter all rooms except the living room were left unheated because of the cost. They felt themselves to be worse off than ever and much poorer than neighbours and members of their family. For them poverty meant 'People going without and (other) people don't realise or don't care. When you go out and say you haven't any money people won't believe you. They think you've got some money in the bank. When you say you haven't got money to buy food today they don't believe you... People do go hungry and get cold. Take elderly people : a lot of them go hungry to keep warm or freeze to eat. There's also a lot more poverty than the Government likes to admit to.' When asked how much they estimated they would need each week to keep out of poverty one said £150 and the other £200. Neither husband not wife now considered they belonged to the working class but to the 'poor' class.

Some of the poorest families encountered in the survey are black families. Unemployment rates are very high in areas where large percentages of the population are black; more blacks than whites are in low paid jobs and some couples with young families have problems over residence qualifications, work permits, bad and overcrowded housing conditions as well as language. Rights under social security are less well known, and as a consequence are less often secured, despite the efforts of organisations working on behalf of ethnic minorities and advice centres. One family with five children in the survey were found to be entitled to over £30 per week in supplementary benefit, and were living on an income far below the state's poverty line.

One parent families have enormous problems in managing on the rates of supplementary benefit. A woman in her mid-thirties, living with her four children aged between 2 and 16 in a council flat in Hackney has been unemployed for several years, and her eldest daughter of 16 is also unemployed. Maintenance payments set at £30 per week are irregular and are included in her total income of £103 per week, which includes child benefit and supplementary benefit but not housing benefit (which covers her rent of £43 per week). She owes a relative £300 and a friend another £200. She has a telephone bill for £89 awaiting payment. The household is very short of facilities and consumer durables. There is no washing machine or refrigerator. There is no spare room for visitors; access to the flat is poor; the rooms are damp and only the living room was heated throughout the winter; there are mice and the flat is in a bad state of interior decoration. Play-space indoors for the two-year-old child is very restricted. There is no garden or other safe place for the child to play safely outdoors. She is not happy about the school meals for the two middle children. 'They have got worse — one sausage and greasy chips is the kind of thing.' These two children do not have raincoats. She and her eldest daughter go without breakfast and she cannot afford two hot meals a day, which she considers to be necessary. She herself does not possess a raincoat and she has only two pairs of stockings. She worries all the time about money, not eating enough, bad housing, the children's future. None of the children could be allowed to go on any outings in 1985. Only one of them had had a holiday away from home. She has looked, and continues to look, 'desperately' for paid work despite the many hours of child care and housework.

Conclusion

It is estimated, on the basis of national data made available by the Government for 1983, but not for subsequent years, that there are at least 300,000 people in London living below the Government's 'poverty line' (or supplementary benefit standard). Another 600,000 receive supplementary benefit, and a further 900,000 have incomes on the margins (with incomes from 1 per cent to 39 percent above that level). The total is 1.8 millions. The present survey is designed to check and explore these numbers to provide better explanations for current trends and produce ideas for policy..

The early findings from the research showed first that there were cases of extreme poverty which were relatively more severe than reported in studies of 10 or 20 years earlier. They applied to unemployed people having difficulty getting benefits at all or regularly, immigrant families and homeless people. Secondly the interviews showed that in important respects current levels of benefit are not 'adequate.' The scale rates payable under the supplementary benefit scheme reflect the Beveridge 'subsistence' standard. The present Government has rejected the principles underlying that standard and has offered no alternative. It is pursuing a strategy to cut the level as well as number of social security payments. The interviews show that those actually living on the benefits are in fact multiply deprived. Both they and the great majority of those who are not poor give higher estimates of the income needed to surmount poverty. The objective evidence about deprivation, including diet, and public opinion in London as a whole suggest that a substantially higher level of basic income is required.

This chapter has also called attention to aspects of the qualitative deterioration in social relations in London. An example is the experiences of claimants in social security offices. Another is the common preoccupation with crime and with personal safety and security in many parts of the city. Many Londoners are deeply concerned about material deprivation and show they want more sweeping measures to deal with it. But they are also concerned that action should be taken to stem the social insecurity which seems to be spreading from the areas of the city which are hardest-hit by

unemployment and by the rundown of incomes of the poorest
wage-earners and social security claimants to many other
communities.

6.

The Feminisation of Poverty

Despite increased access to paid employment on the part of some women and the imaginative policies of some councils, inequality between men and women has in certain respects widened. And within the general percentage increase in the number of people in poverty even more are women than was the case ten or twenty years ago. There are several contributing reasons. The earnings differentials between men and women narrowed in the late 1970s but have now widened again. On the face of it the unemployment rate for men is higher than that for women, but much of the unemployment experienced by women is concealed. Official figures exclude those not entitled to benefit who are actively seeking work. Needless to add, the figures also exclude women who say they would take paid work if opportunities arose locally, and others working part-time who would work longer hours. There is some evidence both that labour market conditions are tending to polarise and that more women than men are experiencing some deterioration in their working conditions, pay or hours. At the more secure and prosperous end of the labour market, for example, there are disproportionate numbers of men. Employer 'fringe' benefits have grown relative to earnings. Moreover, the earnings of higher paid permanent employees have tended to keep further ahead of inflation than those of lower paid employees.

Our attention has been called in the survey to the changes in employment conditions experienced by many women. One woman, aged 38, who had been a catering assistant, drawing a wage of only £63 per week, went to work one day and found a new manager. 'He started paying us (women) in the hand and it worked out less. I tried to look for a better paid job.' She has now been unemployed for nearly a year. Two sisters aged 18 and 19 each receive £393 gross per month, or about £90 per week as clerical assistants in a social security office. They work 38 hours per week. One said 'It's not really what I want to do. There's not much promotion prospects.'

A nursing sister who supervises 60 staff now has a salary of £9,200 gross, or about £140 per week net. She has the care of critically ill people in an intensive care unit of a London hospital. There is heavy lifting, high temperature, noise, and a lot of pressure. She works shifts, often at night. 'The pace and intensity of our work has increased and staff shortages have made some of that increase.' She works very long hours. In the week previous to interview she said she had worked 100 hours.

The work that women do is often reflective of expectations in the home and family. Jobs as nurses, cleaners, laundry workers, cooks, clothing workers, attendants and home helps, for example, have been traditionally jobs filled by women. The status of other jobs filled by women has also been defined in relation to the higher status of men in the home and the difficulties women experience in combining paid work with the care of dependent children, which is still assumed automatically to be their primary responsibility. The skill required in the low paid work which they do is often underestimated, as are the skills exercised in home and family. More couples are today experimenting with shared responsibilities but they remain a small minority.

Some couples who do not have, or no longer have, dependent children are both in paid work and are usually prosperous. This is particularly true of middle-aged couples. Such prosperity has certainly increased, partly because of increased access to paid employment on the part of married women but mainly because of reduced, and earlier, child-bearing and rearing. The number of couples in their mid and late forties who no longer have dependent children in the home has been steadily rising. This means that more women than in the recent past have relatively prosperous living standards.

Paradoxically, however, there has been an increase too at the other extreme. More women also have relatively deprived living standards. There are at least four groups. One group consists of women who look after children or other dependants unpaid and have insufficient income passed on to them indirectly for that purpose. In recent years they have experienced little or no improvement in their financial rights or status, working conditions and in the support they get for some of the arduous tasks they perform. Their male partners have often had working hours reduced and working conditions improved, as well as better fringe benefits and employer welfare, like subsidised midday meals. In the survey we encountered examples in the worst weeks of the winter of 1985-86 of men in low paid employment who nonetheless enjoyed good meals and warm conditions at work while their wives and families skimped on heating and food at home.

The second group consists of women with low earnings in full- or part-time employment who are members of households whose total income falls short of the poverty line, either because the earnings or social security income of other members is small, or because the costs of dependency are high.

The third group are lone women with children. Since 1971 their numbers have nearly doubled to more than a million such families. A majority are in poverty or on the margins of poverty as defined by the rates payable under the supplementary benefit scheme.

The fourth group are elderly women living alone, many of them widows. Between 1961 and 1981 their numbers grew from rather less than a million to over two millions. By 1981 there were nearly 300,000 in Greater London, nearly 130,000 of whom were 75 years of age and over. Some are victims of their former social dependence on husbands and find their resources cut and their isolation difficult to mitigate, especially when they do not have children and grandchildren. Some do not draw supplementary benefit to which they are entitled and are clearly disadvantaged by the deterioration in the administration of social security. The pressure on staff has grown, many offices are unwelcoming and home visits have greatly declined in number. Occupational pension schemes rarely make adequate provision for widows and with inflation decline rapidly in value.

The Government's abandonment in 1979 of the earnings-related formula for the annual uprating of pensions has already led to a substantial reduction in the level which the basic state pension would have reached by 1987 and, according to the Government's own figures in the 1985 Green Paper (Cmnd. 9519, Vol. 3, p.36), the basic pension will halve in value relative to earnings by the year 2033. Given the prospective structure of the population of pensionable age and the likely sources and determinants of their incomes, elderly women will bear the brunt of this decision. The Government is also proposing under the terms of the Social Security Act of 1986 to reduce the scope and value of the additions payable in future under the State Earnings Related Pension Scheme. On the basis of information given to Parliament on 17th January 1986 the largest losses fall on widows, especially those on low earnings. All surveys of the elderly since the war have shown that a high percentage of elderly women are in poverty or on the margins of poverty. Their numbers are growing and the pensions to support them are in some respects worsening.

The Government's strategy in reducing the scope and level of benefits in large parts of the social security system is particularly directed at women (Also see: Land, H. and Ward S., *Women Won't*

Benefit: The Impact of the Social Security Bill on Women's Rights, National Council of Civil Liberties, London, 1986). It seems to be motivated by the belief that women should find support from their menfolk, irrespective of the ability of those men to provide adequate funds, and irrespective of the existing discrimination against women in all of the other resource systems of society.

Government measures outside the social security system are also driving more women into poverty. The 1986 White Paper, 'Building Businesses...not Barriers,' develops the Government's avowed policy of deregulation. It proposes to reduce the number of employees covered by the main employment rights, like protection against unfair dismissal, and rights to maternity and redundancy provisions. This worsens the position of many low-paid employees, and part-time women employees in particular. Even without such proposals Britain is exceptional in Europe in offering poor legal rights to part-time employees, who are treated equally with full-time employees in Austria, Belgium, Denmark, France, Greece, Spain, Norway and the Netherlands. In 1979 the UK Government was alone in the European Community in rejecting a Directive on Voluntary part-time work about minimum rights (Rahman, N., 'Sweeping Aside Women's Rights,' Low Pay Review, No.27, Autumn, 1986, p.12).

Another current illustration of the Government's strategy which is having the effect of accentuating inequality between men and women as well as between rich and poor are its proposals on 'The Reform of Personal Taxation' in a Green Paper. It is proposed to replace the married man's tax allowance with a system of transferable personal tax allowances. While there are many critics of the married man's tax allowance, the Government proposes to make matters worse. New legislation 'would remove ... the present special incentive for two-earner couples...Such positive discrimination is neither necessary nor economically desirable at a time of high unemployment, particularly among the young.' In short, there would be a new incentive for married women to stay at home, and the Government believes that would help to lower the unemployment rate. Single earner couples stand to gain between £11.32 and £19.15 per week, and two-earner couples would receive nothing (The likelihood is that the latter would in fact be taxed more in order to finance a large part of the overall cost and the Government would use part of the savings from the abolition of the married man's tax allowance for selective tax cuts). In other respects the proposals do not begin to fulfil the objective of independence for women, and they also represent, in the spectacular concessions on investment income and capital taxes, a large tax handout to the rich. For example, it is estimated that the disaggregation of investment income will produce a tax cut of over £3,000 per couple for the 11,000 couples earning over £50,000 per year.

Conclusion

A disproportionately large number of the people in poverty in London, as in the country as a whole, are women. There are four main groups: women who look after children or other dependants unpaid and receive insufficient income indirectly for these purposes; lone women with children, whether or not in paid employment; elderly women pensioners, especially those who live alone; and women with low earnings in households in which the earnings or income of others does not enable total household income to surmount the poverty line.

Examples are given of current Government policies dealing with conditions of employment, taxation and tax allowances, social service and social security policies which are tending to enlarge each of these groups.

7.

The Rich, the International Labour Market and Poverty

There is a further source of enlightenment about the position of the poor in London's changing labour market. It is the current employment experience, earnings and living standards and attitudes of rich and prosperous people. For they are involved in the same network of labour market, commercial and service institutions which determines rewards and status. In London the rich are people who hold high international and national as well as city or local status. One person included in our sample is a multi-millionaire from one of the OPEC countries and there are diplomats, traders and others who work in various countries and have homes both overseas and in London. There are also disproportionately large numbers of senior administrative and professional workers. In the London population there are substantial numbers who are well placed in today's conditions. However, what is interesting from our interviews with some of them is the level of recognition of their good fortune, combined with a kind of fatalism or what some would call 'disengagement' suggesting there is nothing they can really do about the poor.

These fatalistic rich people are members of the professions and/ or of powerful organisations, including trans-national corporations. They give an impression of shrugging their shoulders about their own relative affluence in the midst of so much squalor and desperation. What can I do? — each of them seems to be saying. The decisions are being taken out there by people and by organisations so much more powerful than myself. I am just a small cog in a large machine. I just get on with my immediate professional, or administrative or scientific expertise. It is not for me to descend to mere politics. This touches in outline on attitudes held by really prosperous people today. This is the language of their fatalism. It is also the language of their contempt for themselves as much as for the poor. Ironically, it compares unfavourably with the high moral commitment, if censorious condescension, of their Victorian predecessors and represents a kind of betrayal of their social position and power. There are sections of the London population who are doing very well in today's conditions and we are meeting a large number of them.

What is important to grasp is the developing power of that network of relations at the head of the institutions which employ very rich and now also a large number of prosperous people. Increasingly people convey the idea that the organisations for which they, including the richest among them, work are in control of them rather than the other way round. Any full analysis would have to deal with the changing structure of work organisations, including trans-national and national corporations as well as small companies, national and local public services, and professional associations and unions. Recent studies of the labour market show that after mergers and expansion of companies, but also 'rationalisation' after contraction of both companies and public services more ranks have been added to internal hierarchies, making them more unequal, and each rank within the 'permanent' workforce has become more closely defined by legal contracts, fringe benefits and incremental scales. At the same time many of the employing organisations have been creating a much larger number of free-floating lower paid employees (and casual workers in satellite small firms) whose rights are few, indeterminate or non-existent.

The importance of fringe benefits as well as tax allowances in consolidating the advantages of employed elites is still underestimated. 'The differential development of the systems of welfare has played an important but relatively neglected part in the maintenance of both poverty and privilege. The operation of occupational and fiscal welfare outside the welfare state is not only redistributing resources but also power and status upwards' (Sinfield, A., 'Poverty, Privilege and Welfare,' in Bean, P., and Whynes, D., (eds.) Barbara Wootton: Social Science and Public Policy; Essays in her Honour, Tavistock, London, 1986, p.120).

In short, casualisation at one end of the workforce is being matched at the other by status protection and higher rewards. It is vital to establish the exact nature of the structures and the trends taking place in them. Otherwise it will be difficult to understand three things pertinent to this research:- (i) the methods and values by which the number and kind of jobs and the resources available for distribution to employees come to be allocated; (ii) the social relations which exist between employees at different levels of the hierarchy, together with the notions all have about the entitlements and needs of others in the workforce; and (iii) the notions people in employment have about the entitlements and needs of members of the community outside the workplace.

In Chapter 5 (see Table 5.1) evidence was presented of the wider inequality of incomes in London than in Britain generally. Partly this is to do with London being the headquarters for government and many different enterprises, as well as for many international as well as national financial institutions. More people in London now work in banking, insurance and finance than in manufacturing industry. Rewards for some are very high indeed.

'This week Smith New Court financial services group published figures showing that the average basic salary of its directors (excluding the boss) is between £90,000 and £95,000 this year. On top of this they will get at least £40,000 in bonus or commission. The highest paid directors will take home £194,000 this year. The favoured few get much more than this in other firms. Often it is paid in US dollars, and not all of it is taxable.' (McLoughlin, J., 'The City's New Rich,' The Guardian, 6 June, 1986.)

The survey produced a number of examples of rich people working in banking and finance. A 43 years-old company director defined his work as 'advising people how to make money on the commodity market.' He watches TV screens all day long. 'High pressure business is not good for the nerves, because you're advising people how to make money and prices change very quickly, so you have to be alert.' He said he now receives about £1000 per week, or £50,000 per annum, plus £1500 for meals expenses, £2000 pension payments, £2500 life insurance and £450 medical insurance. He had a 'windfall' in the previous twelve months through his association with his company of £175,000. His wife earns £10,000 per annum in a fashion business. They own assets of well over half-a-million pounds: two houses, one in a fashionable part of central London, worth a total of £275,000, company shares worth over £300,000, and nearly £100,000 more in jewellery, antiques, cars, a computer, wine, savings and the encashable value of life assurance. They had taken out a new loan of £100,000 on the rising value of their London home because of the tax relief obtained on the repayments. They had seven weeks holiday in the previous year. They are active members of the Conservative Party and help at elections. Included in their definition of poverty was 'being unemployed and having to survive on state benefits.' While both husband and wife disagreed with the idea that poverty could be diminished more by redistribution than economic growth, and also with the idea of controlling the accumulation of personal wealth, they strongly agreed that the gap between rich and poor was too wide in Britain today and also agreed, though not strongly, that the rich should be taxed more highly.

Among other rich people in the sample was a merchant banker in his thirties who 'offers a view of international financial markets' to clients, and now earns £45,000 per annum but expects promotion to a job with a much higher salary within the next two years. He works 65 hours a week. 'The financial markets have become far more volatile; the nature of the banking business has become more competitive, and has changed the nature of the work.' For someone in his position he took a more orthodox view of Government policy than the company director quoted above. He disagreed with the idea that the rich should be more highly taxed or controlled in other ways and believed that growth was better than redistribution to reduce poverty. However, he estimated that a family like his own, consisting of a married couple with one young child, needed £300 per week to surmount the poverty line.

One theme of current developments in London financial institutions must therefore be of the rich gains for those involved in transactions which are outward looking rather than concerned with investment in British industry. The relative lack of internal investment is well-documented (Bank for International Settlements, Annual Report for 1981; GLC, London Financial Strategy, London, 1986; Minns, R., Take Over the City, Pluto, London, 1982). However, the implications for personal acquaintance or otherwise with low paid employees, whether in the same or in other organisations, and for political attitudes towards domestic issues have not yet attracted much study. Internationalisation has some awkward implications for the acknowledgment of local social responsibility on the part of rich people. Swept into the high finance and quick deals of the whole world they are often uninformed about the poverty being generated in their own city by the financial institutions in which they work. The problem is more than one of a failure to invest in British industry. It is also one of subordinating poorer groups directly to new practices. For example, it has been argued that the financial institutions are 'curbing attempts at self-improvement' and are accelerating 'the decline of the near-poor into absolute poverty by overcharging them and devaluing their savings.' (Toporowski, J., 'Beyond Banking: Financial Institutions and the Poor,' in Golding, P., Excluding the Poor, Child Poverty Action Group, London, 1986).

Among prosperous sections of society the survey produced examples of people equally unaware of the paradoxical connections between institutional wealth and family poverty, unaware too of the low incomes governed by social security payments. But among prosperous people even more than the very rich there were many exceptions to the stock assumptions made about their political and social attitudes, which will bear a lot of examination in the future.

Two contrasting examples will help to convey attitudes. A stockbroker with two teenage children and gross earnings of nearly £30,000, plus substantial pension, car, full pay in sickness, holiday of four weeks and a number of other benefits paid by his firm, believed there were 'only isolated pockets of poverty'. He favoured measures to increase economic growth rather than redistribute income. What he wanted was 'to control the way the poor spend their money'. His wife estimated her total number of working hours per week in the home at 23. Both of them independently said that a family of their size and composition would need £150 to stay out of poverty. This is nearly twice the income payable to such a family in the supplementary benefits scheme.

A bank manager with a wife and two young children earns nearly £20,000 and also obtains considerable indirect additions to remuneration by means of a very low interest housing loan, car, pension, substantial monthly life assurance premiums, and payment of a season ticket from the London suburbs. He felt he was working long hours under a great deal of pressure. The previous week he worked 44 hours and he estimated he spent another 22 hours working in the home and looking after the children and helping an outside voluntary group. His wife did not have a paid job but appeared to work a phenomenal number of hours in the home, looking after her own and others' young children (an estimated total of 120 a week). Both had a sensitive, or educated, understanding of poverty. Asked to say what he meant by the term he said, 'Not having an adequate diet. Not being able to pay for fuel of any kind to heat and cook. Not being able to afford adequate clothing and footwear. Not being able to keep up your health because of insufficient money. Not being able to afford some treat out of the basic routine every three months. People live in poverty if they cannot provide for their children, get together with their family and have a holiday'. He put the poverty line for his family at £200 per week (in fact, at nearly three times the Government's minimum standard). However, he did not think that the gap between the rich and the poor was too wide or that the rich should be taxed more to reduce poverty. He thought that cuts could be made in the NHS without increasing poverty.

In many such examples support for the Government's measures to increase inequality can be found. But there are inconsistencies of attitude which are bound to encourage speculation about the politics of control as much as likely future developments in the structure of society. Thus, Government promotion of the need to cut taxes, reduce (certain kinds of) welfare, expand markets, market capital and the private ownership of shares, housing and other forms of property, finds response a long way down the scale from the wealthiest to those whose prosperity is modest only. Many people in the electorate understand that they are deriving considerable personal benefits from current Government policies. On the other hand, there are a lot of doubts about the loss of different aspects of public welfare. Yes, there are prosperous Christians, professionals and people with Left or Liberal leanings who care about 'decent' living standards for the poor and common access to good housing, education and health care. But there are those who also believe that divisive or sectional policies are in the end self-defeating, because private markets in everything can be inordinately expensive or inefficient, because conflict rather than cooperation is not a prescription for a quiet life, and because present trends pose a threat to personal safety as well as security of individual property. Thus there are doubts which spring from alternative moral and social values, and there are doubts which spring from a belief that a collective price has ultimately to be paid for any lasting personal gain in life. In short, personal prosperity can be guaranteed only by making substantial concessions to collective welfare.

By analysing such examples it becomes easier to interpret recent public opinion polls. A Gallup poll for London Weekend Television found that 71 per cent agreed that the gap between rich and poor is too big and 58 per cent would favour more measures to redistribute money from the rich to the less well-off. Lower but surprisingly substantial percentages of both high income groups and Conservative voters also held these views. But the same poll showed that only a minority of the whole sample thought that anything could be done to close the gap between rich and poor. Most considered it was inevitable. Most people were opposed to specific measures to increase taxation, or limit top earnings and wealth (The Guardian, 25 August, 1986).

Our research is therefore showing the increasingly powerful position of managers, senior administrative staff and professionals connected with the city and with multi-national developments. They protect the interests of the very wealthy and they are living very well themselves. Their prosperity and their attitudes deserve a lot more study. As a class, the very wealthy are also changing in ways which deserve to be better understood. They are more frequently concerned with overseas markets, companies, stockmarkets and trading interests than formerly. What they powerfully contribute to domestic social policy derives in substantial measure from their involvement in the international labour market. Just as the rich entrepreneurs of the first industrial revolution helped to shape Government policies and social relationships in ways very different from the landed gentry, so the corporate managers and professional consultants of transnational companies and agencies represent an equally important new influence upon the national scene.

The International Labour Market

Those who have traced the evolution of the upper classes in British society from the 'feudal baronage' to the business class of latter years point to the importance of new industrial and financial institutions:

> 'The dynamics of the modern capitalist economy are such that those who head the major business enterprises reproduce their own class privileges, and those of their fellow class members, at the same time that they determine the pace and pattern of economic production. The business class remains a propertied class, but its personal wealth is buttressed by the complex structure of 'institutional' ownership which now encompasses so much of the economy. This structure of economic relations is fundamental to the maintenance of the privileges of the business class' (Scott, J., The Upper Classes: Property and Privilege in Britain, London, Macmillan, 1982, p. 186).

The value of undertaking research in London is that the causal importance of internationalism is inescapable. Not long ago London was still the administrative and commercial heart of the largest empire in the world. Because it contained the headquarters of many different national and indeed imperial and later Commonwealth institutions it also contained a disproportionate representation of the richest and most powerful people in the population. They contributed to forms of social extravagance and conspicuous consumption and the overlordship of the advantaged classes which made social stratification in the city rather special. Colonialism no less than extreme wealth also fostered a social distance between classes in London upon which foreign observers were always prone to comment. That structure is now not so much being modified as replaced by European and other international allegiances which perpetuate, and even enhance, that extreme social inequality. The Europeanisation of capital has led to a flight of investment, the abolition of tariffs, a reduction of national measures to assist beleaguered regions and the redeployment of labour forces beyond Europe in the Third World. Those in charge of social policies have been acting in conformity with this development. It is sometimes forgotten that social policies have to be interpreted as paving the way for insensitive and arrogant profit-seeking and not only its correction.

One of the weaknesses of the neo-monetarist position, which is to argue that wage-earners must price themselves back into work, is that there is no logical stopping point before wages plunge to the levels found in the poorest countries of the world. Recent technological developments, and the power of multi-national conglomerates to influence state policies, have combined to make long-distance control of subsidiaries a feasible proposition. In both manufacturing and services London, like Britain as a whole, is being drawn into a more complex international web. Thus transnational companies pay less tax than do other companies. 'A study of 17 of the 20 UK companies in 1982 showed that 14 of them paid no corporation tax at all, as the result of offsets, allowances and declared losses' (Murray, op. cit., p.49).

Social policies of successive Governments, and now of international agencies, cannot be taken at face value. Increasingly in Parliament, as well as in the media, the advocates of these policies are found to be concerned more with public presentation than with structural effect. Often the true effect is misrepresented because only a part of the story which is favourable to the Government is canvassed publicly. This can be illustrated by the urban programme, which in theory should be of vital concern to the redress of the conditions of multiple deprivation documented in the pages above. Between 1979/80 and 1983/84 inner London gained £261m. through the urban programme, but lost over £2000m. through cuts in the Rate Support Grant, reductions in the Housing Investment Programme and cuts in housing subsidies (GLC, Inner City Policy for London; A Fresh Approach, Greater London Council, 1985, p.2). Much the same is true of resources committed to regions with highest unemployment under both national and EEC regional employment programmes. Indeed, the consequence of the shift of responsibility from state to Europe has been to reduce the real value of regional subsidies and spread them more indiscriminately (Armstrong H.W., 'Community Regional Policy: A Survey and a Critique,' Regional Studies, Vol.12, 1978; Townsend P., 'Understanding Poverty and Inequality in Europe', in Walker R., Lawson R., and Townsend P., Responses to Poverty: Lessons from Europe, London, Heinemann, 1984).

Conclusion

This study has already demonstrated two important social trends taking place in the London of the late 1980s:- first, the multiplication and reinforcement of dependency outside the labour market and, second, the casualisation of large reaches of the London economy. This chapter adds a third conclusion, that these trends are matched by conspicuous wealth and rising prosperity at the top end of the market. These trends, like the others, are a by-product of the contemporary developments of financial, industrial and political institutions.

During the late 1980s a large number in the city's population are experiencing unprecedented affluence. Illustrations are given here from our interviews with both very wealthy and prosperous Londoners. The effects upon individual jobs of market trends and government policies in favour of services and banking, insurance and finance are clear. Many of the new rich are involved in international organisations and networks. As such they are distanced from direct acquaintance with some features of London's problems and especially areas of poverty and multiple deprivation. Despite variations of attitude some present themselves as agents of organisations with little or no personal power to influence growing inequality. Some accept that the gap between rich and poor is too wide. Some also accept that that gap deserves to be reduced. On the other hand, there are those whose attitudes towards the poor are arrogant and contemptuous. So while headway might be made among the prosperous classes with at least moderate anti-poverty strategies implacable opposition must be expected from substantial sections, especially the wealthiest and especially those whose labour market situation is most remote from that of severely deprived Londoners.

8.

Alternative Anti-Poverty Strategies

What are the implications of this analysis for policy? The preceding pages provide only a preliminary outline of what will eventually be a substantial detailed account of poverty and the labour market in London. It is perhaps important to acknowledge that there are bound to be themes which have not yet been identified which will have to be added, as well as corrections which will have to be made, to our account. Our purpose in publishing some preliminary findings is to contribute to the continuing debate about policy. The search for better explanations of existing conditions in London has a direct relationship to policy.

There are at least three identifiable alternative strategies. The first is the familiar path of most of the European post-war 'Welfare States'. This is illustrated, for example, in the reports commissioned under the European poverty programme of 1975-80. The policies of each member state of the European Community were described in detail by different authors. In general they achieved a remarkable consensus and in their conclusions recommended more of the same policies. A very helpful review was provided by Joan Brown ('Policies to Combat Poverty', Annex VII to Chapter IV of the Commission's Final Report to the Council on the First Programme of Pilot Schemes and Studies to Combat Poverty, Commission of the European Communities, Brussels, 1981). The reports recognised that poverty was in part due to low earnings and described with approval steps to introduce a national minimum wage and supplement wage income with child benefit. Measures to supplement wages on test of means were accorded less approval. The reports went on to describe social insurance and other schemes to replace employment income for those unable to work because of sickness, disability, old age, child dependancy and involuntary unemployment. Benefits paid as of right were preferred over means-tested benefits, and earnings-related benefits going beyond flat-rate minimum benefits were also approved. The packages of benefits now financed by some European states (Sweden, Denmark, Belgium, Germany and the Netherlands are examples) now account for around a third of Gross Domestic Product, or more than half as much again as countries like Britain (for more detail see Townsend P., 'Poverty in Europe', in Ferge Z. and Miller S.M. (eds.), The Dynamics of Deprivation: a Cross-National Study, for the European Centre for Social Welfare Training and Research, Vienna, London, Gower, April 1987).

The development of post-war strategy had been influenced most by the ideologies of liberal-pluralism. A particularly influential element had been neo-classical economics. People like Keynes and Beveridge had made a lasting impression. In general terms social policy was conceived as being external to the market. Social security for those unable to work and the public social services were to be financed by taxation. The market required a certain regulation, some 'intervention' and different kinds of 'minimum standards' but by and large had to be left to its own devices. The integration or rather equalisation of standards inside and outside work was not really sought, nor was the submission of prosperous sectors of the market to more austere standards so that society in general or the poor might benefit.

We are too close to this ideology to appraise it with any real sense of detachment. Many people of different political persuasion are fiercely attached to some of its most plausible principles. There are also benefits and services dotted around the welfare states of Europe which are thoroughly worthwhile and which few people want to see abandoned. But the events of the 1980s (and the kind of evidence emerging from such research as our survey of London) oblige us to adopt a more critical attitude. The loss of full employment is the key fact in the story.

What has to be concluded from even a cursory review in the mid-1980s, however, is that the consensus strategies of the welfare state, although now being debated quite intensively, remain very powerful and strongly supported in most states, as even Mrs. Thatcher's Government has found. That support is so strong that it is repeatedly being voiced. For example, the International Labour Office undertook a big review of social security during the early 1980s which recommended further developments rather than the abandonment and reconstruction of former institutions and policies. In particular the report reiterated the need to extend benefits as of right (International Labour Office, Into the Twenty-

First Century: The Development of Social Security, Geneva, 1984).

Neo-monetarist Social Policy

What is undeniable is that the debate on welfare has now changed course. Advocates of two alternative strategies, both of which involve a much greater understanding of the markets for goods and labour than was achieved in the post-war consensus, are increasingly making themselves heard. These strategies are not so much new as being newly developed. First, under the continuing influence of the monetarist and neo-classical theories which dominate universities and departments of state alike, there are both mild and severe proposals to dismantle national insurance and universal health and education services. (One extreme example is Minford P., 'State Expenditure: A Study in Waste', Supplement to Economic Affairs, 1984. A less extreme but still severe example is Dilnot A.W., Kay J.A. and Morris C.N., The Reform of Social Security, Institute for Fiscal Studies, Oxford, the Clarendon Press, 1984). The aim is to lift some of the constraints upon a 'free' market and to weaken what are perceived to be obstructive and powerful unions. The highly individualistic orientation of theory suggests that benefits have been too high to foster incentives to get back to work, that there are other people receiving benefits who do not really need them because they have sufficient other resources or could have provided for lean times from their own private resources, and that some unemployed will only 'price themselves back into work' if benefits no longer provide a soft cushion for their inertia. This policy is aimed not only at reducing public expenditure by reducing the costs of social security but is also expected to lower wage costs by increasing the number of people on the labour market who would be prepared to accept work at any , low, price.

To these ends the Government has in fact taken more than 20 different measures since 1979 to reduce the aggregate real cost of social security but has encountered stronger public opposition than had been anticipated. The underlying rationale for the strategy has also found little support. Research studies have not provided much substantiation for the suppositions behind the more sweeping proposals for negative income tax or tax credit and the wholesale abondonment of national insurance. The theory behind these schemes may appear to be mathematically elegant and provide a satisfyingly simple solution to the problems posed by an anomalous and complex structure of benefits but upon examination turns out to be socially and morally vulgar as well as administratively impracticable.

Thus, a careful study of the incomes of the unemployed compared with what their incomes had been at work, described in the trade as 'replacement ratios,' has concluded that 'the financial disincentive to work has been over-stated' (Atkinson A.B. and

Micklewright J., Unemployment Benefits and Unemployment Duration, Suntory-Toyota International Centre for Economics and Related Disciplines, London School of Economics, London, 1985, p.239).

The authors of this study concluded that the overwhelming majority of unemployed get far less income than from their previous or likely prospective earnings; that too little attention has been paid in a lot of slapdash research to the variety of individual circumstances before and after the loss of jobs and to the limitations of micro-data sets for certain types of applied economic research; and, perhaps most important, that too little attention has been given in political and academic analysis to the 'inadequacy of income support for the unemployed' and 'the role of the labour market' (Ibid. pp.237-242). A parallel review of a large number of previous studies concluded that 'the extent of voluntary unemployment was, and is likely to remain, modest indeed' and that the subject 'has absorbed enough of the [economic] profession's resources already' (Micklewright J., Unemployment and Incentives to Work: Policy Evidence in the 1980s, ESRC Programme on Taxation, Incentives and the Distribution of Income, London School of Economics, Discussion Paper No. 92, 1986, p.30)

Corresponding results have been produced from research into tax incentives. The latest available example is from a study carried out by Professor C.V. Brown for the Treasury. 'The survey confirms one common finding of previous work: that tax cuts tend to make virtually no difference to the amount people across the highest band of average incomes want to work...79 per cent of employees could not do any more work in their main job even if they wanted to. Thus tax cuts simply could not have any substantial effect on the supply of labour — on work effort or length of hours' (Huhne C., Economics Editor of the Guardian, 'Treasury Scores Own Goal on Tax Cuts,' The Guardian, 15 December, 1986).

Unfortunately, negative findings from the more reputable corners of the social sciences have not stopped the Government pressing its case and continuing its strategy of cutting and privatising the Welfare State piecemeal. Ironically enough, given the rise in unemployment over the last 10 years, public funds expended on social security have had to increase, despite the severe ideological cuts that have been made, demonstrating the way in which a failure to secure full employment undermines the Government's preferred strategy.

Radical Social Policy

The third alternative strategy has only lately begun to be expressed coherently. The motivation has come from marxist or radical economists, sociologists and social policy analysts. It has also come from politicians working in local councils rather than in Parliament.

It began to emerge in embryonic form early in the 1980s in books and papers about 'the' alternative economic strategy, and involved measures to reconstruct industry and apply a big programme of public investment. This necessarily envisaged radical steps to cut unemployment but also restore the rights of poorer workers and enhance their incomes. This policy approach has been developed within three distinct but interlinked strands: first, a new and more determined approach to the mechanics and politics of the redistribution of incomes; second, the development by local authorities of policies designed to enhance equality of access to local facilities and services; and third, local and national schemes to intervene more effectively in the markets for goods and labour.

More radical proposals for redistribution have been developed by those social policy analysts who have begun to recognise that the limited politics of traditional redistribution are unlikely to allow much further improvement in either the scope or level of benefits, now that the number of unemployed, elderly, disabled and other people dependent on state benefits has grown so rapidly. By the 'limited politics' of redistribution we mean that a political stalemate has been reached between taxpayers and social security claimants because of the limited political definition of the scope of redistribution. Less than half of total household income is now defined by the Board of the Inland Revenue as taxable income. Wealth largely escapes tax, and the development of the wage system, employer fringe benefits and the distribution of wealth is predominantly left to the vagaries of the market or the private sector. It is now time, so the argument proceeds, that society itself decides whether the wage system is becoming too unequal and should be fitted into a framework which includes a publicly defined and sanctioned maximum as well as minimum wage. Similarly, the state should no longer be concerned just with compensation for redundancy, but with the fact of redundancy, or at least have some voice in decisions affecting the redundancy of large numbers of employees. Again, reasonable limits might be fixed to the maximum amount of property or wealth which any single person can inherit, or indeed pass on.

Perhaps the strongest card being played within this philosophical and social approach to redistribution is for a 'basic' or 'social dividend' income scheme. The proposal is not a new one but has been revived in a number of alternative versions in the last few years. The central purpose is to reduce the inequality of incomes between the employed and non-employed. Part of the motivation comes from feminists concerned to ensure that women with little or no access to an income which is theirs by right may obtain a reasonable measure of independence. Another part of the motivation comes from those who are deeply concerned about the income prospects of the long-term unemployed in a 'leisure' society. And part comes simply from those who can see the implications of current social polarisation and do not want to live in a divided or fractured society. The idea may gain momentum if child benefit, pensions and other national insurance benefits, an infant care allowance, a disability allowance and a home responsibility payment, for example, can be seen as practicable political stepping stones towards that goal.

Local government strategies are now recognised to be important to the development of radical national policies. Evidence from London suggests that some of the issues of contemporary polarisation are posing problems on an unprecedented scale for those involved in regional and local politics and administration of services. In 1885, around the time that Charles Booth embarked on his studies of life and labour, London experienced riots. In 1985, both Tottenham and Brixton experienced severe riots (See, for example, the Gifford Report, The Broadwater Farm Inquiry, Report of the Independent Inquiry into Disturbances of October 1985 at the Broadwater Farm Estate, Tottenham, London, 1986). These arose in part from racial disadvantage and harassment but in part from the wider problems of deprivation and instability in the inner city.

Our survey is already producing evidence of widespread concern about threats to personal safety, possessions and property in different London localities. Consequently we should not be surprised that, in a society which is experiencing cuts in the resources available from Government for local services, and is also experiencing highly selective increases in unemployment and therefore cuts in the local economy, the need for new compensatory local social policies is growing. The Archbishop of Canterbury's Commission on urban priority areas called for wider action as well as more sensitive policing. 'There is smouldering anger and quiet despair, and if these are not displaced by hope, overt violence or more destructive activities may surge again, as recent events in Handsworth and Brixton have sadly reminded us' (Faith in the City, 1985, Church House, London, p.348).

This means that local government must involve itself quite explicitly in a wide range of policies that combat polarisation and encourage equality. These have taken many forms, but in London the most important and relevant have been the attempts by a great many authorities to develop and implement equality of opportunities programmes. The best of these cover every aspect of local authority policy and are expressly aimed at increasing the opportunities of both black and other minority ethnic groups and women. Although local authorities cannot overcome inequality, cannot change the market mechanism nor take charge of central government state benefits, they can ensure that their own policies do not actually confirm or reproduce ethnic and gender inequalities and they can influence public opinion in favour of community values. Our preliminary data suggest that inequalities of gender and ethnicity have been growing — interventions by local councils can have a real impact even if they cannot eradicate them.

To be really successful regional as well as local strategies will need to be developed. At regional level 'a new regional administrative structure, based on regional planning boards and regional planning agencies serving regional assemblies' will need to be introduced (Parliamentary Spokesman's Working Group, Alternative Regional Strategy, Labour Party, London, 1983, p.28). In the 1980s the GLC and the six metropolitan councils abolished in March 1986 had begun to demonstrate the huge importance of regional and local strategies to complement, or indeed counteract if necessary, those of Government. The GLC had the powers and resources to act as a major countervailing force. It was following the only path for a humane democracy. The balance has now been tilted towards the powers of the central Government. Without the check provided by the GLC and the six metropolitan councils it will be a lot more difficult for district and borough councils to soften policies which are opposed by a majority of the populations which they represent. This is bound to accentuate existing polarities.

The smaller councils will have to consider how far the uneven growth of deprivation and the uneven access to health and prosperity demands both a more broadly based as well as selective anti-poverty strategy than any they have pursued hitherto, to offset the harm being caused by the effects of current social polarisation, which are documented by this and by other studies. Our interviews illustrate the importance of employment, welfare rights and other ventures for unemployed and otherwise deprived groups. These policies have been vigorously developed in many parts of London. Of particular value in some boroughs are day nurseries, provision of meals and play facilities in school holidays and other local services to families experiencing the worst conditions of long-term unemployment and poverty. Other families in an identical situation in London have not been so fortunate. To many people this difference among the poorest families may not seem much, but that is not how the families themselves see it. Every tangible expression of support to them in a desperate situation is greatly valued. There remains a lot that individual boroughs can do but given restraints imposed by Government that may have to be done more selectively and resources shifted from prosperous to deprived wards.

Finally any overall anti-poverty strategy must take up labour market issues. Both Left and Right agree that without a thriving economy the living standards of some of the population will decline. However, radical strategy as understood on the Left depends on intervening directly in that market. This necessarily involves massive public investment but also direct intervention in sectors of the productive economy to create the right kind of jobs. The scale of legal and financial resources necessary to make any significant impact upon structural unemployment means that only central government can do this job. Local authorities can devise useful models or experiments for others to develop on a larger scale, but lack the resources to make a large impact on unemployment.

In recent years local authorities have proved that they are interested and capable of intervening in their local economies to save and foster employment. The enterprise boards set up by the old metropolitan authorities and the development of an economic policy as exemplified by the GLC's London Industrial Strategy have all shown that the private market can be improved by local authority intervention. By taking shares in or making loans to private companies the Greater London Enterprise Board influenced companies' policies and thus helped to promote goals like unionisation, equal opportunities and socially useful production. Other organisations such as the Greater London Training Board (which in 1985-86 had a budget of £7m compared with an estimated MSC budget of £70m in London) have fought to maintain apprenticeships, develop high quality training schemes in new areas of demand and run schemes for groups known to experience discrimination in the labour market (GLC, London Labour Plan, London, Chapters 12 and 14). Equally directly, local authorities have developed policies of 'Contract Compliance' which use the power of the public purse to tie contractors to certain conditions of pay, work, health and safety and equal opportunities before their tenders can be accepted. Through such policies the labour market can be changed to increase opportunities for disadvantaged groups. Local authorities and other public corporations are of course employers themselves, and they have sought to influence other employers by example — by developing their own equal opportunities policies. Increasingly therefore local government has demonstrated its capacity and power to challenge the way in which the labour market distributes the resources that accrue from different sorts of work. Such policies are beginning to exert more influence over the private sector and hence the extent of deprivation than the more traditional policies dealing with rate-levels and directly provided benefits and services.

Accordingly, local authorities and voluntary bodies can do more than they may realise both to ensure entitlement to income and to provide services and reassurance to those who are most vulnerable to poverty and powerlessness. The answer to poverty lies not just within the powers of Whitehall but within the infrastructure of all our institutions, and therefore, if only to a small extent, within our local political organisations and ourselves.

Conclusion

Three alternative anti-poverty strategies are set out in this chapter. The first is the familiar path pursued by most European 'Welfare States' since the 1939-45 war. This is served by the economic theories and consensus ideologies of liberal-pluralism, whereby there are strong public services and good 'minimum' social security benefits and wages, but as little intervention by Government into the private sector as possible. The strategy is to provide a national minimum standard of living for all citizens within a mixed economy which is nonetheless governed primarily by the edicts of private enterprise.

The second is the alternative strategy being largely pursued by the Thatcher Government — bolstered by the more extreme neo-classical and monetarist economic theories and ideologies. This seeks to privatise public corporations and services, cut public expenditure, reduce guaranteed minima for both social security benefits and wages and, partly by tax cuts, strengthen the powers of the rich. It is also to subscribe to the dictates of the international market. The strategy is to re-introduce unfettered private enterprise and greater social inequality in order to maximise national and personal wealth. The living standards of millions of poor people are more likely to be reduced in real terms under this strategy or, at best, some will have a disproportionately small share of any growth in the economy as a whole.

The third is the alternative economic and social strategy put forward from the Left. It is to reconstitute financial and economic institutions, invest heavily in socially useful employment and effect a radical redistribution of incomes and other resources. Emphasis is placed on the principles of participation and equal access to rights — especially for women and ethnic and other minorities. The strategy differs historically from previous radical strategies in recognising the need to rebuild institutional structures and relationships — in both the public and private sectors, and starting with the labour market, rather than the need only to provide for minimum conditions and standards. The institutions which create or disadvantage the poor at the same time as they create or advantage the rich are the institutions which have to be reconstructed.

9.

Conclusion

This report is based on the early interviews carried out in a representative sample survey in 1985-86 of the population of Greater London and on statistical data currently available, especially evidence about deprivation and mortality in the 755 wards of the city.

In 1987 London's economy is in deeper crisis than it has been for a hundred years. With over 400,000 unemployed the city has the largest concentration of unemployment of any city of the industrial world. Between 1971 and 1981 it lost 36 per cent of the jobs in manufacturing and, by 1985, a total of nearly half-a-million jobs. However, jobs in services have held more or less steady and in banking, insurance and finance they now exceed those in manufacturing. This structural change, compressed into a short span of years, calls attention to London's role as midwife for the development of international banking, insurance and industrial conglomerates. This change also illustrates the problem of growing inequality within the city, with some groups gaining in prosperity and becoming socially more remote while others become more deprived.

The Government's count of unemployment, and especially of unemployment among women, is shown by the interviews to be deficient. If unemployment is applied to people able and wanting to take paid employment, whether full-time or part-time, and not in fact in such employment then the official count does not include three groups which are substantial:-

(i) Men and women who have had a job in the recent past and who have exhausted their right to benefit or who are not entitled to benefit but who want, and can show they have

taken steps to find, paid employment;
(ii) Men under 65 who are receiving an occupational pension and want paid employment;
(iii) Men and women of pensionable age who do not wish to be prematurely retired and want part-time or full-time paid employment.

Unemployment has been growing disproportionately in London wards already worst-affected by unemployment. In some it is between 35 per cent and 40 per cent even on the official, underestimated, count. Other forms of deprivation have been growing disproportionately in these areas too and there is evidence of social polarisation. A wide gulf was found between boroughs in inner London, like Hackney, Tower Hamlets, Islington, Lambeth and Newham, and those in outer London, like Harrow, Sutton, Bexley, Bromley and Havering. We also examined deprivation in all London's 755 wards. Seven of the 25 most deprived were found to be in Tower Hamlets, and another five in Hackney. Three are in Brent and another three in Lambeth. At the other extreme eight of the 25 least deprived wards were found to be in Bromley, another four in Havering and three in Sutton, with the remainder being scattered around the periphery of outer London.

The mortality rate for the young and the middle-aged in the most deprived wards was found to be double, or more than double, the rate in the least deprived wards, and even among those aged 65 and over there continued to be a statistically significant excess.

We found that standards of living among poor and rich are continuing to diverge and are diverging faster in London than in the UK as a whole. A large range of statistical evidence demonstrates the widening of the gap since 1979. The most striking evidence concerns the value of the disposable incomes of the poorest sections of the population. Government survey data can be checked to show that the poorest quarter of the UK population bought less in real terms in 1985 than in 1979. This conclusion applies more sharply to the poorest quarter of the London population.

On the basis of data made available by the Government for 1983, it can be estimated that there are at least 300,000 people in London living below the Government's 'poverty line' or supplementary benefit standard. Another 600,000 receive supplementary benefit and a further 900,000 have incomes on the margins (with incomes from 1 per cent to 39 per cent above that level). The total is 1.8 millions. A disproportionate number of these are women: women who look after children or other dependants unpaid and receive insufficient income; lone women with children, whether or not in paid employment; elderly pensioners, especially women living alone; and women with low earnings in households where total income is low relative to the supplementary benefit rates.

Evidence was found in the interviews of the inadequacy of current rates of social security. Detailed illustrations of families receiving supplementary benefit are given in the text (Chapter 5). They show the extreme difficulties of families with children attempting to live on present rates. In carrying out its review of social security in 1984-85 the Government neither collected evidence to assess the adequacy of benefit rates nor developed an alternative standard to Beveridge's subsistence standard, which they had formally rejected in developing a new system of income support.

We also found that standards of service for social security claimants of all ages have declined seriously. Many people who were interviewed called our attention to the decline generally in the quality of public services and social relations generally in the city, particularly in the most deprived areas. The city's pre-occupation with crime and with personal safety and security is manifest.

Growing dependency outside the labour market and falling wages at the bottom of that market is matched at the top by conspicuous wealth and rising prosperity. Many of the new rich are in banking, insurance and finance, and many are involved in international organisations and networks. Illustrations are given in detail in the text of the circumstances and attitudes towards poverty of such people (Chapter 7). Some are poorly informed and hold contemptuous attitudes. Others believe that the gap between rich and poor is too wide and should be reduced by Government measures.

What action nationally and locally can be taken to meet the problems beginning to be identified in this London research? Three alternative strategies to reduce poverty are briefly reviewed. Neither the predominant strategy of post-war European 'welfare states' nor the reactive strategy of the Thatcher Government are argued to hold much promise of diminishing poverty, or resolving the growing problems of unemployment and social fragmentation and conflict. Only the third, and previously untried, strategy has much prospect of success. This would be to reconstitute existing financial, industrial, labour market and social institutions on the principles of universal and equal access, especially on the part of women and minority groups. It would also be to develop a programme for the redistribution of wealth and income far more radical than any contemplated by successive post-war Governments. And if that programme is to be handled democratically it will depend on a long process of consultation, persuasion and determined political leadership.

Appendix 1
Deprivation

[This is a summary version of a paper published in full in the Journal of Social Policy, April 1987. It was written partly in response to a request from the Board of Science Working Group of the British Medical Association on Deprivation and Disease.]

This paper argues that deprivation is as important a concept as poverty to the analysis of social conditions. It has attracted more and more attention in recent years, but is not yet being treated very coherently. While coherence is never easy to achieve the current scientific and professional literature provides a good basis for review to attempt to improve matters.

The concept has to be distinguished from poverty. People can be said to be deprived if they lack the material standards of diet, clothing, housing, household facilities, working, environmental and locational conditions and facilities which are ordinarily available in their society, and do not participate in or have access to the forms of employment, occupation, education, recreation and family and social activities and relationships which are commonly experienced or accepted (Townsend, 1979, p.413). If they lack or are denied resources to obtain these conditions of life and for this reason are unable to fulfil membership of society they can be said to be in poverty. The first turns on the level of conditions or activities experienced, the second on the incomes and other resources directly available. For purposes of scientific exposition and analysis both ideas have to be clarified.

Objective measures or observations and socially approved conventions do not always coincide. The difference between the two is an important matter for enquiry. The two approaches are explicit or implicit in many studies. There is also a third 'standard' of deprivation. People may not fall below the majority's standard of living but they may fall below what could be the majority's standard — given a better redistribution of resources or a reorganisation of institutions in that society. This last approach tends to be adopted more readily in studies of countries in the Third World than in the First World (Ibid. p.413).

The idea that deprivation takes a variety of forms is widely agreed. A recent review of the entire programme of work on the 'cycle' of deprivation, financed by the Social Science Research Council in the United Kingdom, concluded, 'In using the term deprivation, then, we are essentially referring to the wide range of states or categories of deprivation' (Brown and Madge, 1982, p.39). An earlier study had taken the view that deprivation covers 'all the various misfortunes people can suffer in society.' These involve conditions and experiences 'becoming more unacceptable to society as a whole.... The word deprivation, as it is commonly used, appears to imply a situation that is unacceptably below some minimum standard, even though more general inequality may be accepted as at least inevitable, if not desirable. If inequality can be seen as a hill, deprivation is a ravine into which people should not be allowed to fall' (Berthoud, 1976, pp.175 and 180).

Public concepts of deprivation cannot, however, be understood only according to some scale of scientific discovery and representation. They are socially 'structured' — through a process of familiarity and indifference, advocacy and repetition in social experience and discourse. Interest groups strive to convert them into vehicles carrying their own views and concerns and this can have distorting effects. Concepts like inequality, class, poverty and deprivation may tend to become concepts predominantly about the situation or condition of men than about that of women, especially when put into operational form. Today, any mature consideration of the problems of sexism, racism or ageism, for example, shows that such ideas can be gender-blind, colour-blind or age-blind. The needs of some groups are suppressed in thought and meaning and not simply neglected in fact.

'Material' and 'social' deprivation need to be distinguished. People may not have the material goods of modern life or the immediately surrounding material facilities or amenities. On the other hand, they may not have access to ordinary social customs, activities and relationships. The latter are more difficult to establish and measure, and the two sets of conditions may be difficult in practice to separate (For example, see Bulmer, 1984).

If a primary distinction can be made between material and social deprivation, then sub-categories of both concepts can also be picked out. Some people experience multiple deprivation and others only a single form of deprivation. The pattern must be expected to be paradoxical and uneven. People with prosperous home conditions will be deprived at work, and vice-versa. Some people who are materially deprived will be less socially deprived than their conditions would lead observers to expect.

It follows that scientists must consider deprivation as the darker side of the entire life-style of a people. They have to be aware of all forms of production, consumption, behaviour and status and to consider exclusion or withdrawal from that pattern as a major possible explanation of individual and social pathology. Any specialised examination of a single form of deprivation has to be placed in a more general context of explanation.

'Objective' deprivation in these senses therefore amounts not just to the scientific observation and measurement of events and conditions which are registered on the public's consciousness, but those too which are not. Part of the social scientist's affiliation to 'objectivity' depends on his or her conscious detachment from the social or political consensus developed by state and other institutions. In degree or kind the social scientist must always be on the look-out for what is not yet publicly known or recognised.

Among well-attested scientific work that on the relationship between deprivation and health is particularly persuasive. For many years there has been enormous interest in the relationship between low occupational class and high mortality (See, for recent examples, the Black Report, 1980; Marmot et al, 1984; and Marmot and McDowall, 1986). The same has been true of poor conditions of work and ill-health (One of the latest reviews is that of Joffe, 1985). In the 1980s the literature on the relationship between unemployment and ill-health and mortality has swollen rapidly (For example, Watkins, 1982; Janlert, 1982; Moser, Fox and Jones, 1984; Cook and Shaper, 1984; Fox and Leon, 1985). The work on the correlation between unemployment and suicide by Platt (1982 and 1984) and between low income and high mortality by Wilkinson (1986) is particularly notable. Epidemiologists have also begun to produce evidence of the importance of social relationships and support to health (Berkman and Syme, 1979. See also Broadhead et al., 1983).

Theoretically deprivation can be conceived to be objective, collective (or social) or individually subjective. All three versions of the concept have value in the exposition and analysis of social structure and social change.

Operational Measures

The need for a coherent concept becomes evident once current operational definitions are consulted. A great deal of scientific and statistical work on deprivation has been carried out in the 1970s and 1980s in Britain, much of it concerned with area deprivation and the justification of the selective allocation of resources under various urban aid programmes (See for example, Department of the Environment, 1975a and 1975b; Holtermann, 1975; Coulter, 1978; Millar, 1980; Bentham, 1980; Redfern, 1982; Department of the Environment, 1983; Davies, 1984; Eversley and Begg, 1984; Townsend, Simpson and Tibbs, 1984; Champion and Green, 1985; Greater London Council, 1985; Hayes, 1986). There is little doubt that much of the work was prompted by the growing volume of interest in the use of social indicators for purposes of information, analysis and planning.

It is important to remember that the stock of statistics collected by the state is not necessarily comprehensive or balanced but has grown up piecemeal through history and at each stage has had to secure political rather than scientific approval. The continued exploitation of this limited stock is not necessarily ·the most economical way to proceed in developing studies of deprivation.

Many authorities have already expended huge sums of money on sophisticated computer and other analyses, using a small number of mostly primitive indicators. It is rather like constructing all the most marvellous buildings possible with straw. Investment in the task of producing longer-lasting and more serviceable indicators would be economical in the long run. And of course the Government and many other bodies are incurring huge indirect costs at the present time in relying too heavily on the distorted information conveyed by a few restricted indicators. To give a few examples: there is little or no routinised information on household living standards, income or wealth; individual states of physical and mental health; the type, range and intensity of immediate social, including family, relationships; and the nature and extent of individual work and other activity.

One example of the operational definition of deprivation is the list of eight indicators of urban deprivation put forward by the Department of the Environment (1983). These are:

1. Percent of economically active persons who are unemployed.
2. Percent of households defined as overcrowded.
3. Percent of households with single parent family.
4. Percent of households lacking exclusive use of two basic amenities
5. Percent of pensioners living alone.
6. Percent population change.
7. Standardised mortality rate.
8. Percent of households in which the head was born in the New Commonwealth or Pakistan.

The Department carefully points out that these indicators 'do not cover all facets of urban deprivation. However, it is reasonable to assume that areas which do not appear deprived on the eight indicators examined in this analysis are unlikely to have high overall levels of deprivation' (Department of the Environment, 1983, p.3). That may be true, but it would be reassuring if enquiries in depth were to be made in even a small cross-section of areas in an endeavour to measure 'total' deprivation so that the virtues of different combinations of selected indicators could be evaluated. There is one logical consequence of this procedure which the Department does not appear to examine at all. It is that the use of these eight indicators produces a rather different ranking of areas than does a different number and combination of indicators. This is by no means inconsequential, if only because large grants from the Government are at stake.

This can be appreciated if the tables produced by the Department, comparing different district authorities, are scrutinised. Thus, inner London authorities tend to be ranked highly 'deprived' on indicators of ethnic origin, overcrowding, single parents, household amenities and, to a rather lesser extent, unemployment and numbers of pensioners. On mortality most of them are a long way down the list. By contrast, northern district authorities like Corby, Knowsley, Derwentside, Middlesbrough, Liverpool, Scunthorpe and Hartlepool have dramatically high rates of unemployment and also have high mortality but most of them score low on ethnic minorities, lone pensioners, and lack of exclusive amenities. In recent discussions some local authorities in the North have argued powerfully against their low-ranking on the criteria laid down by the Department of the Environment (See, for example, Hayes, 1986).

Some non-Government measures of deprivation have produced results similar in character. Thus, in an important series of papers Professor Jarman constructed 'underprivileged area scores' for each of the 9265 electoral wards in England and Wales and then combined them to make up sets of information about family practitioner committee areas, comparing the results with assessments by general practitioners of their workload (Jarman, 1983 and 1984).

Slightly or substantially different lists of indicators, with different weightings, have been preferred in other studies (See, for example, Davies, 1984; Scott- Samuel, 1983; Department of Planning and Design, Sheffield, 1983; Eversley and Begg, 1984; Townsend, Simpson and Tibbs, 1984; GLC, 1985; Thunhurst 1985a and 1985b). It is evident from the various studies that more attention needs to be given to the justification of the indicators chosen — or their 'coherence'.

Indicators of deprivation are sometimes direct and sometimes indirect, sometimes representing conditions or states and sometimes representing victims of those conditions or states. From a sociological perspective it is important to distinguish between the measurement of deprivation in different areas and the kind of people experiencing that deprivation. Otherwise there is a danger of treating age, ethnicity and single parenthood as causes of the phenomenon under study. It is wrong in principle to treat being black or old and alone or a single parent as part of the definition of deprivation. Even if many such people are deprived it is their deprivation and not their status which has to be measured. And many people having that status are demonstrably not deprived.

A related problem is to try to counter bias in the selection of 'objective' or material indicators and the emphasis given to groups of them in the overall index. Measures used socially tend to be 'structured.' They can be unwittingly discriminatory, as for example by gender or colour. This can happen if more of the selected items in the measure of deprivation apply to men than to women or cover the situation of whites better than blacks.

In the text above one attempt to meet some of these problems within the limits of available statistics has been to define material deprivation in terms of four indicators;- unemployment; overcrowding; lack of resources (not owning a car); and also lack of resources (not owning or buying a home). As listed at the end of this report all 755 wards in Greater London have been ranked according to these four indicators, as have all 678 wards in the Northern Region of England in another recent study (Townsend, Phillimore and Beattie, 1986).

A Measure of Multiple Deprivation

A more elaborate attempt to meet the problems of defining multiple deprivation operationally has been developed in our interviews. Two general points should be explained. First, it was assumed that in principle the items listed in any definition of material and social deprivation should represent all aspects of the material and social conditions of life. For various, mainly practical, reasons, it is impossible to apply this principle comprehensively, although it is possible to cover large areas of experience in interviews which are prolonged.

Second, it was assumed that the definition should be 'objective' rather than subjective : the items to be selected were to be indicators of conditions, relationships and behaviour rather than of attitudes or beliefs, important though it may have been to establish independently the nature of those attitudes or beliefs against which conditions and behaviour could be compared. Again, this principle is difficult to fulfil in interview conditions.

The types of deprivation covered by the survey questionaire were as follows:

Material Deprivation	Social Deprivation
Dietary	Rights to employment
Clothing	Family activities
Housing	Integration into community
Home facilities	Formal participation in social institutions
Environment	Recreation
Location	Education
Work (Paid and unpaid)	

A list of 77 indicators or groups of indicators was developed to reflect types of deprivation under these headings and is summarised below. The results will be described in subsequent reports. The list of 77 indicators or groups of indicators include a number which are based on international practices (e.g. indicators on safety at work and poor conditions at work recommended by the OECD) and others drawn from previous national surveys by Government and non-Government investigators, and all appear, from scrutiny of the early questionnaires completed by interviewers, to be valid (in the sense that in every case they reflect the conditions, experience and activities of a statistical majority of the population). Two further points should be emphasised. The sample interviewed in Greater London were invited for most of these indicators to say whether or not they believed them to be 'necessary in today's conditions', that is, necessary to them as individuals. Majority opinion on the elements believed to be necessary to present-day living standards can therefore be compared with majority circumstances and behaviour. Second, the interviews include a large number of questions about forms of subjective deprivation. The relationship between objective and subjective deprivation can therefore be extensively explored.

An Illustrative Index of Multiple Deprivation

A distinction was drawn between material and social deprivation and a division was made into 13 specific types of deprivation. A total of 77 indicators or groups of indicators were selected (with a total maximum score of 94). These are set out below:-

Material Deprivation:

1. Dietary deprivation:
  i. At least one day in last fortnight with insufficient to eat;
  ii. No fresh meat or fish most days of week (alternative formulation for vegetarians);
  iii. No special meal or roast most weeks;
  iv. No fresh fruit most days;
  v. Short of food on at least one occasion in last 12 months to meet needs of family;

2. Clothing Deprivation:
  i. Inadequate footwear for all weathers;
  ii. Inadequate protection against heavy rain;
  iii. Inadequate protection against severe cold;
  iv. No dressing gown;
  v. Fewer than three pairs socks/stockings in good repair;
  vi. Bought second-hand clothing in last 12 months;

3. Housing Deprivation:
  i. No exclusive use of indoor WC and bath;
  ii. External structural defects;
  iii. Internal structural defects;
  iv. No electricity;
  v. All rooms not heated winter evenings;
  vi. Housing not free of damp;
  vii. Housing not free of infestation;

  viii. Poor state of internal and/or external paintwork and decoration;
    ix. Poor access to accommodation;
     x. Overcrowded (fewer rooms — excluding kitchen and bathroom — than persons);
    xi. No spare room for visitor to sleep;

4. Deprivation of home facilities:
     i. No car;
    ii. No television;
   iii. No radio;
   iv. No washing machine;
    v. No refrigerator;
   vi. No freezer;
  vii. No electric iron;
 viii. No gas or electric cooker;
   ix. No vacuum cleaner;
    x. No central heating;
   xi. No telephone;
  xii. Lack of carpeting in main rooms;

5. Deprivation of Environment:
     i. No garden;
    ii. Nowhere for children under five to play safely outside;
   iii. Nowhere for children aged five to ten to play safely nearby;
   iv. Industrial air pollution;
    v. Other forms of air pollution;
   vi. Risk of road accidents around home;
  vii. Problem of noise from traffic, aircraft, building works;

6. Deprivation of Location:
     i. No open space (like park or heath) within easy walking distance;
    ii. No recreational facilities for young people or older adults nearby;
   iii. No shops for ordinary household goods within 10 minutes journey;
   iv. Problem of litter in local streets;
    v. Doctor's surgery or hospital outpatients department not within 10 minutes journey;

7. Deprivation at Work:
     i. Poor working environment (polluted air, dust, noise, vibration and high or low temperature — maximum score of 9);
    ii. Stands or walks about more than three-quarters of the working day;
   iii. Works 'unsocial hours';
   iv. Either poor outdoor amenities of work;

or poor indoor amenities at work (maximum score of 10);

7a. Alternative series on Deprivation at Work:

(for people not answering questions applying to paid employment and who have shown they undertake at least 20 hours unpaid work altogether caring for children, sick or disabled or elderly persons in the household or elsewhere):

   i. Repeat the total score for housing deprivation (item 3 above — maximum score of 11);

   ii. No central heating (4 x. above: repeat score if necessary);

   iii. No telephone (4 xi. above: repeat score if necessary);

   iv. Worked 50 or more hours in last week (Unpaid work but also including any paid work).

   v. Air pollution (items 5 iv. and 5 v. above)

   vi. Repeat the total score for locational deprivation (item 6 above — max. score 5).

Social Deprivation:

8. Lack of Rights in Employment:

   i. Unemployed for two weeks or more during previous 12 months;

   ii. Subject to one week's termination of employment or less;

   iii. No paid holiday;

   iv. No meals paid or subsidised by employer;

   v. No entitlement to occupational pension;

   vi. Not entitled to full pay in first six months of sickness;

   vii. Worked 50 or more hours previous week;

9. Deprivation of Family Activity:

   i. Difficulties indoors for child to play;

   ii. If has children, child has not had holiday away from home in the last 12 months;

   iii. If has children, child has not had outing during the last 12 months;

   iv. No days staying with family or friends in previous 12 months;

   v. Problem of the health of someone in family;

   vi. Has care of disabled or elderly relative;

10. Lack of integration into community:

   i. Being alone and isolated from people;

   ii. Relatively unsafe in surrounding streets;

   iii. Racial harrassment;

   iv. Experiences discrimination on grounds of race, sex, age, disability or sexual orientation ;

   v. In illness no expected source of help;

   vi. Not a source of care or help to others inside or outside the home;

vii. Moved house three or more times in last five years;

11. Lack of Formal Participation in Social Institutions:
  i. Did not vote at last election;
  ii. No participation in trade union or staff association, educational courses, sport clubs or associations,or political parties;
  iii. No participation in voluntary service activities;

12. Recreational Deprivation:
  i. No holiday away from home in last 12 months;
  ii. Fewer than five hours a week of specified range of leisure activities;

13. Educational Deprivation:
  i. Fewer than 10 years education;
  ii. No formal qualifications from school or subsequent educational courses or apprenticeships.

Material and Social Deprivation: Total indicators or groups of indicators: 77 (with a maximum total score of 94).

Appendix 2
Poverty

[This appendix summarises work related to that in this report in two recent sources: Townsend P., (1985), 'Basic Needs', in Kuper A. and Kuper J. (eds.), The Social Science Encyclopedia, London, Routledge and Kegan Paul; and Townsend P., (1987), 'Conceptualising Poverty' in Ferge Z. and Miller S.M. (eds.), The Dynamics of Deprivation: A Cross-National Study, London, Gower Press.]

The meaning of 'poverty' is being debated in the late 1980s more keenly by social scientists than at any time. Partly this is because of increasing use of the term to describe conditions in poor as well as rich societies. When applied in these contexts the word has tended to take on different meanings and, correspondingly, methodologies of measurement and modes of explanation have also tended to differ. For example, books on poverty in the 'Third World' are often more critical, and theoretically more radical than those about poverty in the first world. Compare recent studies such as those of Hayter, 1981; Hoogvelt, 1982; and even less radical accounts of Third World problems such as the Brandt Report, 1980; or Fields, 1980; with the comparative analysis provided by the European Commisssion, 1981; or the earlier statistical study by the OECD, 1976; as well as the work of individual scholars like Beckerman et al, 1979a; and 1979b; Berthoud and Brown with Cooper, 1980 and Hagenaars, 1985.

The dissimilarity in the literatures is fascinating and clearly owes a lot to the particular perspectives of the social scientific traditions of individual nation states as well as the differing ideologies and intellectual backgrounds of the peoples undertaking the studies. Such contrasting references illustrate two things. They certainly illustrate the subtle influence of ideology upon meaning. But they also call attention to the failure thus far to treat 'poverty' consistently as a scientific phenomenon with universal application. (For a fuller account of the differences to be found in the literature see Townsend, 1984, 1985 and 1986).

For many generations the idea of poverty has attracted strong intellectual and political interest (see Himmelfarb, 1984, and Woolf, 1987, for extensive historical analysis). As long ago as 1834 'the mischievous ambiguity of the word poor' was a dominant theme of the Poor Law Report. At the present time there can be said to be three alternative conceptions of poverty which are conventionally established or professionally supported and which offer a basis for international or comparative work. These depend on conceptions respectively of (i) subsistence; (ii) basic needs; and (iii) relative deprivation.

Subsistence

In the nineteenth century, governments and ruling groups found it necessary to confront the problems of defining the needs of the poor in terms of income. For centuries under the old Poor Laws parishes had developed varying forms of indoor and outdoor relief for the poor. Economies newly based on manufacturing industry and an incentive wage system posed new problems of regulating the amounts to be received by the poor outside as well as inside Poor Law institutions. The costs of maintaining institutions and their inmates had given concern to ruling groups and in the formulation of a new scheme to manage the poor from 1834 in Britain, for example, the principle of 'less eligibility' played a crucial part in the thinking both of politicians and those undertaking scientific enquiries.

> The first and most essential of all conditions, a principle which we find universally admitted, even by those those practice is at variance with it, is, that [the paupers'] situation on the whole shall not be made really or apparently so eligible as the situation of the independent labourer of the lowest class. (*Report ... of the Poor Laws*, 1834, p.228)

The ratepayers wanted the costs of maintaining the able-bodies and non-able-bodied poor kept as low as possible and those in charge of the economy as well as employers wanted the poor to be prepared to accept the lowest wage rates on offer. Sometimes relief was offered in terms of bread and other benefits in kind. Sometimes small sums of cash were added and sometimes cash formed the sole form of relief for the non-institutionalised poor. The management of a modern industrial state invited rationalisation of methods and amounts of relief.

For these various reasons, then, there was pressure to define the minimum needs of institutional inmates and the able-bodied poor outside institutions. The early work of nutritionists in Germany, the United States and Britain was addressed to such questions. In Germany, for example, this has been documented in the work of Kuczynski and Zuntz (see Leibfried, 1982; and see also Hoffmann and Leibfried, 1980). In the United States the work of Aronson (1984) is particularly authoritative. There were powerful attempts to restrict the living standards of the poor for reasons of rising costs for the ratepayer and the taxpayer, as well as the costs to the employer of wage labour, but these motivations were complicated by public debates, and scientific enquiries, about the 'needs' of the poor. Towards the end of the nineteenth century and early in the twentieth century methods were explored of legitimating the relative living standards of inmates of institutions, and both the employed and non-employed poor living outside institutions. It is now easier to trace some fo the ways in which science has served political interests.

In Britain, the 'subsistence' standard came to fruition in two stages: first towards the end of the nineteenth century by means of surveys carried out by entrepreneurs like Rowntree (1901 and 1918) and then in the second world war by means of a report on social security drawn upon by Sir William, later Lord, Beveridge (Beveridge, 1942). Under the old Poor Laws the needs of the poor had been measured in terms of quantities of bread or bread-flour and the cash equivalent, and in some parishes allowances for other necessities became common practice. (See *Report ... of the Poor Laws*, 1834, p.22). This tradition was clarified by investigators like Charles Booth and Seebohm Rowntree. Families were in poverty when their incomes were not 'sufficient to obtain the minimum necessaries for the maintenance of merely physical efficiency' (Rowntree, 1901, p.86). A family was treated as being in poverty if its income minus rent fell short of the poverty line. The poverty line was defined in the 1890s for a family of married couple and three children as 12s 9d a week for food, 2s 3d for clothing, 1s 10d for fuel and 10d for household sundries, making 17s 8d altogether, with actual rent in addition. The standard also played a big part in discussions about minimum wage rates (see, for example, Rowntree, 1918).

The formulation by Rowntree and others at the turn of the century played a substantial part in the thinking about the welfare state legislation of the Liberal government in the first years of the twentieth century. The formulation was adopted in the second world war by Beveridge in drawing up plans for a reorganisation of social security after the war. The particular interpretation by Beveridge of 'subsistence' was carried over into the post war years as a means of justifying the low rates of national assistance and national insurance benefits. Although the rates of benefits have been increased in the years since the war because of inflation there has been no subsequent investigation officially sanctioned to review the principles under which 'minimum' benefit rates should be defined — not even in the major review of social security in 1984-5, as explained above. This illustrates the major importance of the subsistence standard in Britain.

The standard has also played a substantial part in the management of poverty in other socieities. During the history of the British Empire and then the British Commonwealth the idea of subsistence was freely exported from Britain to member states. The wages of blacks in South Africa are partly legitimated according to the 'poverty datum line' (Pillay, 1973; Maasdorp and Humphreys, 1975). In framing development plans, former colonised territories (eg. India and Malaysia) still draw heavily on the subsistence conceptualisation (India, 1978, 1985; Malaysia, 1976). In the United States 'subsistence' remains the lynch-pin of the government's measures of poverty (US Department of Health Education and Welfare, 1976). It would be difficult to exaggerate the historical and contemporary significance therefore of the use of the idea of 'subsistence' in formulating views about the extent of poverty in the world and developing policies to alleviate the condition.

The use of 'subsistence' to define poverty has been heavily criticised (Rein, 1970; Townsend, 1979). The chief criticism is that human needs are interpreted as being predominantly physical needs — that is, for food, shelter and clothing — rather than as social needs. People are not, it is argued, simply individual organisms requiring sustenance for physical existence. They are social beings expected to perform socially demanding roles as workers, citizens, parents, partners, neighbours and friends. They are not simply consumers of physical goods but producers of those goods and participants in complex social associations. Such criticism carries greater force than mere amendment of the formulation of the 'subsistence' standard. For example, the amount as well as the type of food we eat depends on the social roles we play and the dietary customs we observe as well as the kinds of food made available socially. 'Subsistence' needs can therefore be redefined within a broader social conceptualisation. (For further exposition of the discussion among social scientists, see Piachaud, 1981 and Townsend, 1981; Sen, 1983 and 1985; Townsend, 1985; and Desai, 1986).

Basic Needs

A second formulation has been actively taken up in recent years in the discussion about conditions in the poorest countries of the world. This is the 'basic needs' formulation. In reports produced by international agencies the term has a long history (see, for example, Drewnowski and Scott, 1966). But the term was given particularly wide currency after the International Labour Office's World Employment Conference at Geneva in 1976, where it was formally adopted. Basic needs were said to include two elements:

> Firstly, they include certain minimum requirements of a family for private consumption: adequate food, shelter and clothing, as well as certain household furniture and equipment. Second, they include essential services provided by and for the community at large, such as safe drinking water, sanitation, public transport and health education and cultural facilities ... The concept of basic needs should be placed within a context of a nation's overall economic and social development. In no circumstances should it be taken to mean merely the minimum necessary for subsistence; it should be placed within a context of national independence, the dignity of individuals and peoples and their freedom to chart their destiny without hindrance. (ILO, 1976, pp.24-25)

The concept of 'basic needs' has played a prominent part in a succession of national plans (see, for example, Ghai *et al*, 1979) and in international reports (see, UNESCO, 1978; and the Brandt Report, 1980). The term is quite clearly an enlargement of the subsistence concept. Despite the rhetoric like that in the quotation above it differs only in the additional emphasis on minimum facilities required by local communities. However, the element of arbitrariness in the additional items incorporated in the concept is even more transparent and the criteria by which the choice is made are not clearly laid out. The needs of populations cannot be defined adequately just by reference to the physical needs of individuals *and* the more obvious physical provisions and services required by local communities. The exposition of need depends on assumptions which have to be made about the functioning and development of societies. The emerging *social* expectations laid upon the citizens of poor countries during periods of development are not adequately acknowledged. The disproportionately greater poverty and deprivation experienced by ethnic minorities, women, the elderly, children and people with disabilities in such countries is not adequately allowed for in this formulation.

It is important to recognise the function of 'basic needs' in the debates going on about the relationship between the first and third worlds. The more that social aspects of needs are acknowledged, the more it becomes necessary to accept the relativity of need to the world's as well as to national resources. The more the concept is restricted to physical goods and facilities the easier it is to argue that economic growth alone, rather than a complex combination of growth, redistribution and reorganisation of trading and other institutional relationships is implied.

Relative deprivation

For the reasons given some social scientists have been turning to a more comprehensive and rigorous social formulation of the meaning of poverty. Societies are passing through such rapid change that any standard devised at some historical date in the past is difficult to justify in new conditions. People living in the present are not subject to the laws and obligations as well as customs which apply to a previous era. There are, therefore, major problems in merely updating any historical benchmark of poverty by some index of prices. Over many years the 'relativity' of meanings of poverty has been recognised in part if not comprehensively. Adam Smith, for example, recognised the ways in which 'necessities' were defined by custom in the early part of the nineteenth century. He gave the instance of the labourer's need to wear a shirt (Adam Smith, 1812). Some of those who have sought to modernise previous applications of the 'subsistence' standard have felt obliged to make similar concessions to a relativist perspective. Thus Seebohm Rowntree widened his 1899 definition when he came to repeat his survey of poverty in York in 1936 to include newspapers and trade union subscriptions. However, the concessions have been made more unconsciously than consciously and have been applied only fragmentarily to the scientific measurement of need. Others, like the European Commission, have adopted a 'relativist' starting point but have found themselves unable, perhaps because of disagreement among specialists, to move from a general to an operational definition (Commission of the European Communities, 1981, p.30).

Poverty must not be described by reference only to relative disposable income. Some analysts have used an operational definition of the poorest ten per cent or twenty per cent of the population, as defined by a criterion of disposable income. (In its 1985 Green Paper on Social Security the Government also fell back on this convention for illustrative purposes). This is to fail to distinguish conceptually between inequality and poverty. The latter concept may best be understood as applying not just to those who are victims of a mal-distribution of resources but, more exactly, to those whose resources do not allow them to fulfil the elaborate social demands and customs which are placed upon citizens of that society in the first place.

Poverty may therefore be defined in relation to the idea of 'relative deprivation'. People are relatively deprived if they cannot obtain, at all or sufficiently, the conditions of life — that is, the diets, amenities, standards and services — which allow them to play the roles, participate in the relationships and follow the customary behaviour which is expected of them by virtue of their membership of society. If they lack or are denied resources to obtain access to these condition of life and so fulfil membership of society they may be said to be in poverty. People may be deprived in any or all of the major spheres of life — at work where the means largely determining position in other spheres are earned; at home, in neighbourhood and family; in travel; in a range of social and individual activities outside work and home or neighbourhood and in performing a variety of roles in fulfilment of social obligations.

As with any formulation, there are problems in defining poverty operationally. Under the 'relative deprivation' approach a threshold of income is conceived, according to size and type of family, below which withdrawal or exclusion from active membership of society become disproportionately accentuated. But because people lead different roles during their lives and engage in different associations, detailed and comprehensive scientific observation is necessary to demonstrate both the extent and severity of non-participation. In one type of society families may no longer be able to go on even the cheapest holiday, or invite friends to their homes, or send their children to school when money has to be provided for some special function or outing. Old age pensioners may fail to join friends in a club or a pub because they lack the resources to share the costs. In another type of society families displaced, say, by changes in land tenure and the extension of plantation farming may become dispersed on poorer land and find they have insufficient resources (whether in cash, produce and other goods and services to exchange) to secure loans or services and play a significant part in the local community. Lacking a sufficient role their poverty becomes compounded.

Within families the social effects of deprivation may be selective or concentrated. Or individuals may maintain some aspects of their social lives (as within their families) at the expense of withdrawing totally or almost completely from other forms of social association. Again, the failure to observe a *socially* adequate diet may take different forms. We are at a relatively early stage of the recognition of the *social* needs of individuals and the full social effects of low income remain to be systematically described and scientifically investigated, but this is not an unfamiliar stage in the evolution of scientific definition and theory.

Appendix 3
Changes in Household Disposable Income of Rich and Poor

at constant (1985) prices (£ per week)

Year	Greater London			
	Lowest Decile	Lower Quartile	Upper Quartile	Highest Decile
1983	60.66	88.65	254.20	359.27
1984	50.27	86.87	257.97	368.07
1985	46.60	89.50	261.51	367.82
Percentage Change 1983-85	−23.2	+1.0	+2.9	+2.4
Year	United Kingdom			
1979	53.59	85.92	220.80	297.43
1981	57.73	86.98	227.89	304.71
1983	57.99	86.84	220.57	301.93
1984	49.75	83.80	226.57	307.72
1985	48.44	83.45	232.74	322.59
Percentage Change 1979-85	−9.6	×.9	+5.4	+8.5

Source: Department of Employment (1980-86) *Annual Reports of the Family Expenditure Survey*, London, HMSO.

Appendix 4
Multiple Deprivation Ranking

Ranking of GLC Wards on a Multiple Deprivation Index, Calculated from 4 Indicators

Ward Name	Borough	Zscore Index	Unemployment	Overcrowding	Renting	No Car	Total H'holds
Spitalfields	Tower Hamlets	8.42	21.95	28.26	96.47	79.64	1925
St. Mary's	Tower Hamlets	6.92	19.49	16.53	95.18	74.01	1990
Carlton	Brent	6.46	21.71	10.31	97.60	77.05	2911
Colborne	Kensington and Chelsea	6.41	19.14	13.21	93.12	73.71	2589
Shadwell	Tower Hamlets	6.29	17.28	14.09	98.10	71.27	2846
Blackwall	Tower Hamlets	6.28	21.15	11.44	97.54	68.73	2034
Haggerston	Hackney	6.28	18.00	13.23	97.29	72.09	2401
St. Katherine's	Tower Hamlets	6.12	15.45	15.68	97.06	69.01	3498
White City & Sheph	Hammersmith and Fulham	6.05	17.65	12.37	88.73	74.33	3817
Kings Park	Hackney	6.05	19.26	11.52	97.80	68.09	2642
Ordnance	Newham	6.00	22.56	9.21	97.59	67.51	1989
Angell	Lambeth	5.92	18.81	10.53	93.30	72.31	4300
Westdown	Hackney	5.84	18.85	12.32	84.38	67.08	1940
St. Dunstan's	Tower Hamlets	5.80	18.41	9.99	97.70	71.12	2997
Liddle	Southwark	5.73	18.62	9.66	99.38	69.43	4185
Harrow Road	Westminster	5.70	15.45	12.59	88.74	72.60	4521
Eastdown	Hackney	5.64	17.09	11.38	90.87	68.40	3438
Queen's Park	Westminster	5.63	16.73	10.49	91.42	73.09	3891
Stonebridge	Brent	5.60	16.80	12.77	83.52	66.71	2239
Rectory	Hackney	5.60	18.98	11.10	80.03	67.52	3270
Larkhall	Lambeth	5.59	17.70	11.72	84.67	66.76	4919
Avondale	Kensington and Chelsea	5.56	16.97	11.44	85.13	69.41	2973
Weavers	Tower Hamlets	5.54	16.09	10.24	96.66	71.79	3444
Vassall	Lambeth	5.52	18.36	9.97	89.96	74.04	4306
Westbourne	Westminster	5.45	15.55	10.57	88.30	74.04	4306
Latchmere	Wandsworth	5.41	15.89	10.62	90.14	70.46	4067
Bromley	Tower Hamlets	5.41	16.76	9.76	96.57	68.30	3178
St. Raphael's	Brent	5.37	17.30	12.25	82.87	61.73	3497
Roundwood	Brent	5.37	15.73	13.47	77.99	65.34	2613

Ferndale	Lambeth	5.37	17.71	11.07	77.26	67.56	4481
Limehouse	Tower Hamlets	5.31	17.73	9.07	95.58	65.96	3190
Marlowe	Lewisham	5.26	17.72	8.50	95.60	68.48	3318
St. Peter's	Tower Hamlets	5.18	15.34	9.30	95.71	70.37	3797
Chaucer	Southwark	5.17	13.83	10.37	96.28	71.04	3733
Beckton	Newham	5.16	19.95	7.96	97.13	60.74	2752
Abbey	Southwark	5.15	15.05	8.98	98.59	70.95	2405
Church Street	Westminster	5.09	13.86	8.98	97.07	75.49	3863
Gibbs Green	Hammersmith and Fulham	5.08	13.45	12.48	82.22	68.41	2885
Chatham	Hackney	5.08	16.63	8.89	91.06	66.93	3367
Friary	Southwark	5.06	16.03	8.95	90.86	68.51	3075
Colville	Kensington and Chelsea	5.06	16.58	8.97	80.59	71.46	2865
Thornhill	Islington	5.05	16.64	8.63	89.39	68.28	2545
Brownswood	Hackney	5.04	16.37	9.20	82.78	69.43	3130
St Pancras	Camden	5.04	14.94	8.43	95.73	72.90	1969
Northwold	Hackney	4.99	17.21	9.88	77.17	64.81	3289
Burgess	Southwark	4.97	14.87	9.42	95.77	66.16	2527
Oval	Lambeth	4.96	15.80	9.15	87.94	67.20	4460
Stockwell	Lambeth	4.95	13.98	10.83	89.31	67.23	4331
St. John	Wandsworth	4.94	14.93	10.02	84.44	67.71	4459
Grinling Gibbons	Lewisham	4.87	18.26	7.40	91.22	64.18	3303
Moorfields	Hackney	4.85	13.87	8.42	96.30	72.09	2568
Wenlock	Hackney	4.84	14.56	7.78	98.54	71.54	2610
Springfield	Hackney	4.79	16.50	10.27	72.56	63.20	3425
Tollington	Islington	4.78	16.83	7.76	84.39	67.87	3851
Earls Court	Kensington and Chelsea	4.76	11.39	14.73	71.44	68.19	3701
King's Cross	Camden	4.75	16.01	6.50	90.13	75.50	2166
Somers Town	Camden	4.74	12.36	8.07	98.14	77.70	2318
Milwall	Tower Hamlets	4.73	17.11	8.47	95.92	57.32	3651
Queensbridge	Hackney	4.71	15.78	8.00	90.34	65.81	3086
Custom House & Sil	Newham	4.64	17.04	9.30	86.46	55.75	3730
St. Charles	Kensington and Chelsea	4.63	13.95	9.08	88.78	66.17	2148
Evelyn	Lewisham	4.60	15.74	6.71	94.61	68.80	3486
Kilburn	Camden	4.60	15.81	8.37	78.92	66.61	3861

Ranking of GLC Wards on a Multiple Deprivation Index, Calculated from 4 Indicators

Ward Name	Borough	Zscore Index	Unemployment	Overcrowding	Renting	No Car	Total H'holds
Kilburn	Brent	4.59	13.23	10.82	74.96	67.47	3606
Brunswick	Southwark	4.59	14.50	7.79	92.49	67.93	3969
Highview	Islington	4.58	15.03	9.02	82.89	63.68	1917
South Stanley	Kensington and Chelsea	4.54	14.78	8.27	83.99	66.97	2342
Lansbury	Tower Hamlets	4.50	15.33	6.93	95.98	65.89	2910
Addison	Hammersmith and Fulham	4.50	14.03	9.08	77.38	68.30	2997
Northfield	Hackney	4.50	16.23	8.58	75.02	63.44	3230
Dalston	Hackney	4.50	16.06	7.34	82.74	66.90	3030
East India	Tower Hamlets	4.47	15.28	7.34	95.50	63.23	2465
Leabridge	Hackney	4.45	15.92	9.26	71.04	62.38	3187
Castlehaven	Camden	4.44	16.31	6.92	84.94	65.83	2038
Victoria	Hackney	4.43	16.01	6.65	92.20	65.18	3848
Browning	Southwark	4.42	14.19	6.42	98.90	70.67	4004
College Park & Old	Hammersmith and Fulham	4.42	13.06	9.30	83.34	66.41	2978
New River	Hackney	4.42	14.05	8.35	85.62	65.67	3943
Grafton	Camden	4.38	14.28	7.44	89.75	66.78	2391
Dockyard	Southwark	4.37	14.50	7.40	97.89	62.56	3267
Bishop's	Lambeth	4.37	12.56	7.13	97.06	72.79	3710
South Defoe	Hackney	4.37	16.81	7.68	73.50	63.98	2083
Clissold	Hackney	4.36	14.86	9.11	73.49	63.40	3406
St. Giles	Southwark	4.34	15.59	6.84	86.34	65.89	4224
Kensal Rise	Brent	4.33	15.02	13.44	54.51	57.54	2106
St James'	Tower Hamlets	4.33	14.78	6.28	96.08	68.12	2550
Holy Trinity	Tower Hamlets	4.32	12.84	7.45	97.58	67.87	3064
Wilesden Green	Brent	4.31	14.53	13.01	55.87	59.06	2690
Stratford	Newham	4.30	14.03	8.91	77.56	64.10	2447
Courtfield	Kensington and Chelsea	4.29	10.37	15.29	72.35	60.07	3211
Tulse Hill	Lambeth	4.28	16.91	8.25	66.43	62.28	4301
Mapesbury	Brent	4.27	12.42	10.61	77.97	62.52	3300

Canning Town & Gra	Newham	4.27	15.75	7.89	81.46	60.02	2993
Harlesden	Brent	4.25	13.98	11.94	62.09	59.46	2403
St. Andrew's	Brent	4.23	14.61	11.41	68.83	54.86	2752
Bricklayers	Southwark	4.23	14.55	5.90	97.93	68.31	2751
St. George's	Islington	4.23	14.97	7.09	81.80	66.26	4456
Coningham	Hammersmith and Fulham	4.18	12.68	9.56	74.20	65.45	4050
Consort	Southwark	4.17	14.67	6.28	88.89	67.54	2485
Holloway	Islington	4.15	13.40	6.83	92.32	67.23	3660
Prince's	Lambeth	4.12	12.65	7.02	90.98	69.40	3635
Caversham	Camden	4.12	14.76	6.33	85.24	67.46	2527
De Beauvoir	Hackney	4.11	13.47	7.85	86.77	62.58	3289
Plashet	Newham	4.09	14.32	11.05	63.89	56.76	3963
Goresbrook	Barking and Dagenham	4.07	12.11	10.58	95.77	52.13	2504
Nightingale	Greenwich	4.07	16.39	6.27	99.92	55.05	1229
Faraday	Southwark	4.04	13.08	6.67	97.75	64.47	4877
Cathedral	Southwark	4.03	16.33	4.54	95.75	68.17	2824
Clerkenwell	Islington	4.02	12.11	6.60	95.58	69.88	3574
Bayswater	Westminster	4.01	12.43	7.37	80.21	70.85	4290
Town Hall	Lambeth	4.01	14.34	7.98	76.37	61.12	4985
White Hart Lane	Haringey	3.99	14.67	7.89	81.26	57.65	3576
Seven Sisters	Haringey	3.98	14.29	8.16	71.12	62.41	2476
Avonmore	Hammersmith and Fulham	3.98	12.12	9.14	74.91	64.77	2794
Newington	Southwark	3.90	13.12	5.98	95.70	66.33	3811
Redcoat	Tower Hamlets	3.88	12.55	6.41	94.91	65.86	2592
Sussex	Islington	3.88	13.77	7.39	75.20	64.09	2246
Pepys	Lewisham	3.87	14.76	7.49	76.59	58.87	3887
Kelfield	Kensington and Chelsea	3.87	13.36	7.60	77.85	62.87	2659
Riverside	Southwark	3.86	12.66	5.68	98.43	68.41	3059
Canonbury East	Islington	3.85	14.02	6.19	88.39	63.29	2653
Northcote	Ealing	3.85	14.91	32.67	24.06	42.57	3067
Little Venice	Westminster	3.84	11.10	8.27	89.81	63.44	3993
Arsenal	Greenwich	3.84	14.03	5.97	90.96	63.13	1272
West	Greenwich	3.82	13.59	6.64	85.97	62.46	2366
Lancaster Gate	Westminster	3.81	9.59	12.86	68.85	62.16	3885

Ranking of GLC Wards on a Multiple Deprivation Index, Calculated from 4 Indicators

Ward Name	Borough	Zscore Index	Indicators				Total H'holds
			Unemployment	Overcrowding	Renting	No Car	
West Ham	Newham	3.81	13.33	8.68	72.36	59.12	2836
Junction	Islington	3.76	13.70	6.59	80.44	63.49	3431
Wick	Hackney	3.75	13.16	6.32	89.90	62.83	3307
Barset	Southwark	3.73	18.92	5.21	73.44	57.99	2221
Pembridge	Kensington and Chelsea	3.72	9.83	11.21	70.32	63.82	3336
Mildmay	Islington	3.71	13.18	5.27	91.82	68.31	3056
Camden	Camden	3.68	13.84	6.76	77.77	61.44	2308
Plaistow	Newham	3.67	14.41	7.83	65.19	59.78	3373
Cambell	Barking and Dagenham	3.66	11.13	9.35	95.54	52.30	3518
Bow	Tower Hamlets	3.63	12.72	6.29	92.96	60.87	2828
Sherard	Greenwich	3.61	12.71	8.01	95.00	50.95	2621
Clapham Town	Lambeth	3.58	13.41	7.00	75.72	60.39	4460
Burnt Oak	Barnet	3.57	11.54	8.90	80.10	56.55	4774
Regent's Park	Camden	3.57	11.34	6.33	88.82	67.14	3793
Gillespie	Islington	3.56	13.93	7.75	61.76	61.55	2220
South Hornsey	Haringey	3.55	13.96	7.88	65.51	58.58	2615
Hillmarton	Islington	3.54	12.25	5.99	84.95	66.30	2937
St. Mary's Park	Wandsworth	3.53	12.08	8.06	78.02	58.04	4126
Park	Tower Hamlets	3.53	13.57	4.80	97.49	63.65	2352
Eel Brook	Hammersmith and Fulham	3.53	12.28	8.70	69.50	58.48	2485
Fieldway	Croydon	3.53	12.51	9.72	94.34	44.21	3126
Alibon	Barking and Dagenham	3.52	13.12	8.82	72.40	53.20	2279
Cathall	Waltham Forest	3.52	13.50	7.60	68.49	59.31	4094
Barnsbury	Islington	3.51	12.95	6.45	80.77	61.49	3552
St. James	Westminister	3.50	17.52	3.37	86.59	66.49	1544
North Defoe	Hackney	3.50	13.51	8.74	62.16	56.93	1649
Park	Newham	3.47	13.79	8.97	59.08	56.13	3558
St. Mary	Islington	3.47	11.88	6.36	82.62	64.98	3038
Upton	Newham	3.45	13.93	13.80	42.09	50.81	3167

Queenstown	Wandsworth	3.44	12.39	7.24	78.17	58.99	3134
Normand	Hammersmith and Fulham	3.44	10.98	7.64	77.22	63.63	2708
Park	Haringey	3.42	13.57	6.84	72.92	58.55	2603
Bedford	Wandsworth	3.38	12.60	8.26	67.75	56.82	5364
Glyndon	Greenwich	3.38	13.98	5.64	76.80	61.45	2185
Rotherhithe	Southwark	3.37	10.69	6.51	98.15	60.70	3076
Bloomsbury	Camden	3.36	8.86	7.05	85.63	73.18	2442
Heathfield	Ealing	3.36	12.51	6.94	73.22	60.64	5318
Churchill	Westminster	3.31	9.99	5.85	90.15	70.77	4002
Millbank	Westminster	3.30	9.96	5.13	92.92	75.34	3178
Grove	Tower Hamlets	3.30	12.97	6.64	70.67	60.53	1807
Valence	Barking and Dagenham	3.29	12.09	7.54	76.94	55.92	3539
High Cross	Haringey	3.27	12.65	7.80	69.89	55.37	2464
Hillrise	Islington	3.26	13.65	5.62	75.32	60.73	3525
Wormholt	Hammersmith and Fulham	3.26	11.70	7.90	67.11	59.95	3366
Bunhill	Islington	3.25	10.47	4.70	99.11	71.94	3491
St. John's	Camden	3.25	13.50	5.58	73.44	62.39	2455
Grove	Hammersmith and Fulham	3.24	13.84	6.14	67.70	60.21	2690
Dormers Wells	Ealing	3.24	13.54	12.06	59.70	42.43	4025
Highbury	Islington	3.23	13.28	5.56	73.86	62.84	3650
St. Mary's	Greenwich	3.21	15.04	2.89	99.16	68.46	2394
Homerton	Hackney	3.18	13.29	8.04	57.33	56.92	2339
New Town	Newham	3.16	12.71	6.76	69.36	58.41	2115
Tottenham Central	Haringey	3.16	12.48	7.54	63.85	58.07	3967
St. Stephens	Newham	3.14	12.12	11.91	45.99	53.30	2392
Bellingham	Lewisham	3.14	11.05	6.66	80.68	57.67	3167
Quadrant	Islington	3.13	13.20	4.84	80.96	60.16	2810
The Lane	Southwark	3.12	12.79	5.37	80.96	60.16	2810
Glebe	Ealing	3.12	12.16	24.04	30.50	41.66	3830
Fairfield	Wandsworth	3.11	11.98	7.77	67.82	55.95	3042
St Martin's	Lambeth	3.10	11.41	6.55	81.71	57.67	4533
Gospel Oak	Camden	3.10	11.65	4.88	85.37	66.31	2502
Walham	Hammersmith and Fulham	3.09	10.72	6.97	75.24	61.41	2670
Roehampton	Wandsworth	3.07	10.33	7.03	94.25	54.42	4676

Ranking of GLC Wards on a Multiple Deprivation Index, Calculated from 4 Indicators

Ward Name	Borough	Zscore Index	Unemployment	Overcrowding	Renting	No Car	Total H'holds
Kensington	Newham	3.07	12.47	14.11	38.08	50.68	2432
Margravine	Hammersmith and Fulham	3.06	9.08	9.28	71.46	59.79	1745
South Tottenham	Haringey	3.04	13.29	8.89	50.17	54.85	2597
Broadway	Hammersmith and Fulham	3.04	10.17	4.87	88.98	71.32	2033
Noel Park	Haringey	3.02	12.11	5.75	74.23	61.26	4156
Fanshawe	Barking and Dagenham	3.00	10.51	8.21	75.72	54.06	3192
Thamesmead Mooring	Greenwich	3.00	13.46	6.30	94.60	45.03	1758
Brondesbury Park	Brent	2.99	11.30	7.51	72.01	55.36	3569
Herne Hill	Lambeth	2.99	13.02	6.49	64.98	57.36	4269
Sands End	Hammersmith and Fulham	2.99	11.95	6.38	68.55	60.30	2162
Maida Vale	Westminster	2.93	11.45	5.37	84.00	60.18	3500
Queens Park	Brent	2.92	10.51	9.29	62.50	54.50	2400
West End	Camden	2.91	12.25	6.10	68.97	58.77	2688
Earlsfield	Wandsworth	2.90	12.36	8.57	59.23	51.25	3245
Holborn	Camden	2.89	9.50	4.24	95.00	74.40	2619
Castle	Newham	2.87	12.46	7.80	57.51	54.52	2770
Leyton	Walton Forest	2.87	12.73	6.38	65.09	56.31	4294
Drake	Lewisham	2.85	12.67	5.76	70.96	56.84	4063
Swiss Cottage	Camden	2.84	10.95	6.53	72.69	58.50	4365
St. George's	Westminster	2.82	9.33	6.82	76.30	62.88	4034
Chalk Farm	Camden	2.80	17.13	5.03	61.89	50.70	2086
Manor	Brent	2.78	12.39	9.52	48.93	51.30	2532
Hudsons	Newham	2.78	13.51	5.99	65.19	53.73	3671
Triptons	Barking and Dagenham	2.76	11.45	7.08	69.67	53.11	3446
Parsloes	Barking and Dagenham	2.76	9.68	7.08	89.24	52.78	2556
Wembley Central	Brent	2.75	11.20	13.95	40.90	47.62	2560
Thames	Barking and Dagenham	2.69	13.12	4.96	89.21	49.34	2420
Manor	Barking and Dagenham	2.69	10.44	6.61	75.95	55.64	2437
Lyndhurst	Southwark	2.69	11.53	5.165	75.01	56.83	4198

Burrage	Greenwich	2.66	14.59	5.07	65.95	52.89	1401
Church End	Brent	2.65	10.62	10.81	48.18	51.75	2221
Bruce Grove	Haringey	2.63	13.86	7.27	48.25	52.80	3938
South	Newham	2.55	12.46	5.91	66.41	52.85	3367
Brook Green	Hammersmith and Fulham	2.54	10.58	6.30	64.83	59.01	2855
Abbey	Barking and Dagenham	2.51	11.55	7.53	57.53	52.02	3200
Hither Green	Lewisham	2.48	12.42	5.79	62.62	54.11	4056
West End	Westminster	2.46	7.57	5.92	80.76	68.96	2297
St. Peter	Islington	2.46	10.66	4.13	81.17	64.22	3706
Forest Gate	Newham	2.45	12.11	7.39	51.60	52.76	3684
Coleraine	Haringey	2.44	12.06	6.39	58.26	53.83	4025
St. Alfege	Greenwich	2.43	11.74	4.78	79.23	54.37	2600
Clapham Park	Lambeth	2.41	11.02	6.24	66.17	53.88	4996
Middle Park	Greenwich	2.41	10.70	6.12	89.93	46.26	2632
Tooting	Wandsworth	2.39	9.79	8.74	52.55	54.98	5081
Higham Hill	Waltham Forest	2.39	11.19	7.81	65.47	46.01	2343
Eastbury	Barking and Dagenham	2.38	11.46	5.67	77.91	49.59	2327
Brunswick	Camden	2.38	6.47	5.67	80.67	78.45	1640
Central	Newham	2.37	10.22	11.14	38.38	54.18	2561
Ferrier	Greenwich	2.37	10.90	5.86	84.58	47.90	2613
Gascoigne	Barking and Dagenham	2.36	11.91	3.81	89.22	55.63	3618
Harringay	Haringey	2.36	11.44	8.71	44.14	52.93	3675
Eynsham	Greenwich	2.31	12.24	4.60	74.21	51.32	2572
Victoria	Westminster	2.28	11.02	3.37	81.50	65.51	1930
Waverley	Southwark	2.28	11.87	5.33	65.73	53.39	2833
Churchdown	Lewisham	2.27	10.39	6.85	66.52	50.56	3937
Thamesmead East	Bexley	2.25	12.32	5.44	78.02	45.32	3644
Streatham Hill	Lambeth	2.25	11.27	4.87	71.63	55.44	5262
St. Helier South	Sutton	2.25	8.33	6.30	87.20	53.92	1953
Goodmayes	Redbridge	2.24	11.42	8.05	56.70	45.80	3702
Penge	Bromley	2.24	10.74	6.51	62.94	51.95	3840
Baker Street	Westminster	2.22	6.83	6.31	80.39	66.13	2234
Craig Park	Enfield	2.21	11.13	5.91	64.03	52.50	2811
Mount Pleasant	Ealing	2.21	11.14	19.21	32.12	36.12	3696

Ranking of GLC Wards on a Multiple Deprivation Index, Calculated from 4 Indicators

Ward Name	Borough	Zscore Index	Unemployment	Overcrowding	Renting	No Car	Total H'holds
Charlton	Greenwich	2.20	13.03	5.56	59.63	49.47	2284
Vale	Ealing	2.19	9.77	7.69	61.54	50.30	2535
Shaftesbury	Wandsworth	2.18	10.02	5.78	67.84	55.47	5072
Brompton	Kensington and Chelsea	2.17	8.42	7.86	66.22	53.40	1412
Woolwich Common	Greenwich	2.16	11.25	4.58	80.04	52.05	2465
Little Ilford	Newham	2.15	11.73	6.45	53.90	51.58	3889
Pymmes	Enfield	2.13	11.53	5.81	65.31	49.32	3082
Bellenden	Southwark	2.12	10.98	5.19	61.83	56.79	4338
Starch Green	Hammersmith and Fulham	2.12	9.97	6.87	55.27	55.34	2200
St. James Street	Waltham Forest	2.12	11.70	7.22	47.79	51.13	4570
Manor Park	Newham	2.11	10.93	7.88	48.26	50.78	3732
Downham	Lewisham	2.08	9.16	5.80	76.28	53.48	3950
Trafalgar	Greenwich	2.08	10.82	4.46	72.38	56.32	2578
Gipsy Hill	Lambeth	2.07	11.14	4.83	73.58	51.58	4311
Cannonbury West	Islington	2.06	10.45	3.71	82.42	59.43	2508
Balham	Wandsworth	2.01	10.28	6.53	57.64	52.19	4547
Hornsey Central	Haringey	2.00	10.59	4.66	68.11	56.45	2832
West Hill	Wandsworth	1.98	9.58	7.33	68.42	45.62	3138
Lavender	Merton	1.98	10.07	6.12	68.97	49.00	1943
Monega	Newham	1.97	11.24	11.52	30.04	48.65	2483
Thornton	Lambeth	1.96	10.29	6.06	60.31	52.20	3268
Hornsey Vale	Haringey	1.96	11.13	6.28	56.08	49.88	2452
South End	Camden	1.96	10.96	4.37	65.39	57.47	2424
Hyde Park	Westminster	1.93	9.85	6.16	65.36	50.34	2907
Church	Kensington and Chelsea	1.92	7.58	5.10	74.76	64.72	2159
Belsize	Camden	1.92	8.83	6.10	62.82	56.82	3886
Graveney	Wandsworth	1.89	9.33	6.82	55.07	54.13	4739
Abingdon	Kensington and Chelsea	1.89	9.12	7.15	59.08	51.25	3050
West Green	Haringey	1.89	11.25	5.94	49.98	53.39	4292
Sherbrooke	Hammersmith and Fulham	1.88	10.82	4.95	59.18	55.66	2102

Ward	Borough						
St. Helier North	Sutton	1.87	8.36	5.01	80.74	56.48	3535
Nightingale	Wandsworth	1.89	10.02	6.54	52.17	53.10	4982
High Street	Waltham Forest	1.82	9.86	5.80	58.12	54.04	4432
Hoe Street	Waltham Forest	1.78	10.30	5.92	52.77	53.70	4389
Cricklewood	Brent	1.76	9.80	8.00	48.02	48.42	3074
Redcliffe	Kensington and Chelsea	1.73	9.42	5.81	61.76	52.19	3342
St. Leonard's	Lambeth	1.72	9.36	6.36	59.11	50.77	4339
Rectory Field	Greenwich	1.72	11.96	3.80	69.13	51.10	2582
Sydenham East	Lewisham	1.71	10.20	4.70	70.05	51.10	3956
Springfield	Ealing	1.69	9.02	6.35	60.21	51.26	4614
Adelaide	Camden	1.67	9.94	4.71	69.61	51.52	3613
Forest Hill	Lewisham	1.65	9.92	5.42	64.17	49.43	2618
Green Lanes	Haringey	1.64	10.85	5.85	46.40	53.14	2802
Colehill	Hammersmith and Fulham	1.64	9.93	4.98	58.45	54.94	2609
New Addington	Croydon	1.64	9.26	8.35	69.77	37.88	4082
Marks Gate	Barking and Dagenham	1.63	9.83	5.09	98.24	39.35	1080
Hornfair	Greenwich	1.63	10.54	3.95	76.77	50.53	2355
Parkside	Wandsworth	1.61	8.93	6.25	75.80	43.94	3199
Cann Hall	Waltham Forest	1.61	10.97	6.10	46.66	50.50	3770
Hilldene	Havering	1.61	11.32	4.31	73.51	45.87	3462
Cavendish	Westminster	1.60	6.66	5.46	76.33	60.54	2801
Rushey Green	Lewisham	1.60	10.75	4.25	56.63	56.74	3152
Leytonstone	Waltham Forest	1.60	10.79	6.23	47.66	49.60	4205
Blackheath	Lewisham	1.59	10.01	4.93	71.49	47.49	2413
Anerley	Bromley	1.58	10.01	5.11	64.59	49.40	4053
Ladywell	Lewisham	1.58	10.82	5.39	53.65	50.01	3614
Hounslow Heath	Hounslow	1.58	8.90	11.23	48.51	38.90	3688
Herbert	Greenwich	1.56	12.04	4.76	60.73	45.21	2814
Lloyd Park	Waltham Forest	1.55	9.93	5.36	54.49	52.92	4483
Chamberlayne	Brent	1.54	10.24	7.94	42.97	46.27	2895
Bryanston	Westminster	1.52	7.06	5.25	70.45	60.32	2267
Whitefoot	Lewisham	1.52	10.68	5.44	58.72	46.45	2689
Whitehorse Manor	Croydon	1.52	9.37	6.68	52.74	48.86	5059
Cranford	Hounslow	1.51	8.68	11.58	55.35	34.98	3456

Ranking of GLC Wards on a Multiple Deprivation Index, Calculated from 4 Indicators

| Ward Name | Borough | Zscore Index | Indicators | | | | Total H'holds |
			Unemployment	Overcrowding	Renting	No Car	
Streatham Wells	Lambeth	1.49	10.13	4.95	60.75	50.00	4989
Grove Park	Lewisham	1.48	10.33	4.41	70.71	47.73	2561
Woodside	Haringey	1.48	10.45	5.90	50.01	49.01	3591
Town	Hammersmith and Fulham	1.48	9.80	4.39	62.09	54.45	2754
Broad Green	Croydon	1.46	9.46	6.64	50.70	48.63	4696
Gunnersbury	Hounslow	1.41	9.11	4.88	68.83	49.67	4045
Knight's Hill	Lambeth	1.40	10.64	4.91	58.08	47.92	4363
Colindale	Barnet	1.38	7.89	9.19	60.27	40.03	5140
Norbiton	Kingston Upon Thames	1.38	8.66	5.42	64.19	49.98	3119
Uxbridge South	Hillingdon	1.37	10.10	5.00	61.88	46.98	2201
Bowes Park	Haringey	1.36	9.99	5.41	51.21	50.58	4421
Colliers Wood	Merton	1.29	9.30	6.78	48.31	47.03	3082
West Hendon	Barnet	1.25	8.99	8.66	47.18	41.26	4926
Gooshays	Havering	1.20	10.71	4.68	64.00	42.79	3900
Heath	Barking and Dagenham	1.19	9.54	5.37	65.73	42.57	3671
Isleworth South	Hounslow	1.19	8.85	5.80	66.94	42.71	3760
Highgate	Camden	1.17	10.22	3.33	70.13	50.93	4115
Village	Barking and Dagenham	1.09	9.68	3.86	73.72	45.99	3649
Heaton	Havering	1.09	10.66	4.80	62.16	41.31	4210
Sulivan	Hammersmith and Fulham	1.07	8.69	4.35	61.97	52.01	2393
Ravenscourt	Hammersmith and Fulham	1.07	7.48	4.48	65.42	54.19	2288
Victoria	Ealing	1.04	9.67	7.47	41.81	42.62	2478
Sydenham West	Lewisham	1.00	8.48	4.94	69.87	44.35	3807
Furzedown	Wandsworth	0.97	9.00	5.64	51.04	46.68	5092
Alleyn	Southwark	0.97	9.24	4.72	53.04	49.78	2694
Angel Road	Enfield	0.97	9.74	4.27	50.20	52.21	2787
Queens Gate	Kensington and Chelsea	0.95	7.12	6.94	54.39	47.45	2826
Wall End	Newham	0.94	8.98	7.76	36.26	46.44	3891
Fitzjohns	Camden	0.94	7.80	5.32	60.32	48.64	2311

Wood Street	Waltham Forest	0.94	9.56	4.31	55.95	48.94	4527
Turnham Green	Hounslow	0.94	9.01	4.17	57.43	51.62	3766
West Putney	Wandsworth	0.93	8.44	4.47	68.86	46.47	5106
Townfield	Hillingdon	0.93	8.73	5.31	64.64	42.33	3900
Lakedale	Greenwich	0.93	9.79	5.65	39.93	49.73	2389
Holland	Kensington and Chelsea	0.89	8.21	6.09	55.53	44.22	3303
Northcote	Wandsworth	0.89	8.21	6.09	55.53	44.22	3303
Fortune Green	Camden	0.87	10.55	4.01	51.31	48.16	2099
Lea Bridge	Waltham Forest	0.84	9.05	5.31	42.57	51.27	4254
St. Peter's	Enfield	0.83	10.49	4.23	47.12	48.70	3425
Hounslow West	Hounslow	0.81	9.07	9.81	36.84	37.21	3681
Yiewsley	Hillingdon	0.78	8.99	5.66	60.13	39.23	2370
Loxford	Redbridge	0.77	10.15	7.65	29.42	44.97	4014
Ealing Common	Ealing	0.77	8.13	4.99	58.03	46.93	4765
Plumstead Common	Greenwich	0.76	10.89	5.14	40.43	44.74	1264
Bemersyde	Newham	0.75	8.87	5.35	40.88	51.59	2353
Phipps Bridge	Merton	0.75	8.26	4.04	63.15	49.55	3639
Campden	Kensington and Chelsea	0.74	7.50	5.22	54.47	50.31	3068
Valentines	Redbridge	0.72	9.55	5.74	40.89	45.80	3903
Grove Green	Waltham Forest	0.70	8.60	5.48	41.45	50.70	4285
Heston West	Hounslow	0.70	8.09	8.28	59.00	32.82	3795
Elthorne	Ealing	0.70	8.95	5.48	43.16	47.75	4361
Crouch End	Haringey	0.65	8.61	4.65	53.72	46.96	3764
Southfield	Wandsworth	0.64	8.67	4.61	49.35	49.23	5183
Mottingham	Bromley	0.61	7.75	4.45	65.47	45.81	3750
Forest	Waltham Forest	0.58	9.31	5.68	40.17	45.13	3943
Springfield	Wandsworth	0.57	8.63	3.92	61.49	46.22	4832
Manor Lee	Lewisham	0.50	9.98	3.79	49.42	46.51	2825
River	Barking and Dagenham	0.45	9.15	7.86	31.10	41.31	2354
Hobbayne	Ealing	0.44	8.49	5.68	47.37	41.77	4121
Childs Hill	Barnet	0.42	8.55	4.76	51.62	43.62	4965
North End	Bexley	0.41	8.31	4.12	65.93	41.82	3786
Crofton Park	Lewisham	0.41	9.23	4.24	46.28	46.87	4058
East Putney	Wandsworth	0.40	7.51	5.23	54.76	44.02	5141

Ranking of GLC Wards on a Multiple Deprivation Index, Calculated from 4 Indicators

Ward Name	Borough	Zscore Index	Indicators				Total H'holds
			Unemployment	Overcrowding	Renting	No Car	
Crabtree	Hammersmith and Fulham	0.40	7.50	4.52	49.11	51.52	2144
City of London	City of London	0.40	7.00	2.95	95.10	46.33	2001
Tokyngton	Brent	0.39	9.01	11.43	21.83	39.58	3692
Hans Town	Kensington and Chelsea	0.37	7.89	3.90	57.42	48.45	3025
Barham	Brent	0.34	8.90	8.63	29.61	39.38	3857
Wandle Valley	Sutton	0.34	7.46	5.84	54.12	40.67	1833
Royal Hospital	Kensington and Chelsea	0.31	7.43	3.96	55.62	50.25	1769
Southfield	Ealing	0.30	8.60	4.16	46.10	48.34	4564
Erith	Bexley	0.29	10.42	3.63	48.70	42.81	3702
Hamilton Terrace	Westminster	0.29	7.30	3.36	60.61	52.84	2884
St Nicholas	Greenwich	0.29	9.77	5.44	37.58	41.54	2629
Bothwell	Hillingdon	0.27	7.65	6.08	51.84	38.83	2369
Colham	Hillingdon	0.27	8.31	5.24	64.33	34.76	2369
West End	Ealing	0.26	8.61	4.80	62.67	36.07	4187
Brentwater	Brent	0.25	8.25	8.90	28.87	40.38	2889
Thamesfield	Wandsworth	0.24	8.54	3.22	55.05	49.40	5402
Hanworth	Hounslow	0.24	7.64	6.02	63.05	34.15	3691
East Finchley	Barnet	0.23	7.49	5.02	49.89	44.88	5434
Rye	Southwark	0.22	8.21	3.81	55.96	45.59	3281
St. Helier	Merton	0.21	7.45	3.25	64.78	49.30	3509
Regent's Park	Westminster	0.19	6.72	3.78	59.68	51.45	4256
St. Paul's Cray	Bromley	0.15	8.74	4.32	56.14	38.98	5688
Kidbrooke	Greenwich	0.14	8.96	3.24	61.92	42.33	2563
St. Margaret	Lewisham	0.13	7.91	2.83	63.76	49.59	2828
Waddon	Croydon	0.13	7.42	5.00	50.26	43.55	5163
Ponders End	Enfield	0.12	8.99	5.04	41.06	41.51	3395
Enfield Wash	Enfield	0.11	8.57	5.25	46.84	38.67	3160
Hounslow	Central	0.10	8.13	8.36	28.91	40.28	3168
Chiswick Homefield	Hounslow	0.10	8.12	3.49	52.16	48.33	3016

Name	Borough						
Argyle	Ealing	0.09	8.20	4.68	48.41	41.91	4834
Chase Cross	Havering	0.07	9.10	6.81	48.62	30.03	2649
Ravensbury	Merton	0.03	7.12	4.22	56.62	44.64	3389
Oldchurch	Havering	0.03	8.83	5.31	38.99	40.68	2503
Walpole	Ealing	0.03	8.43	4.44	41.23	45.72	4979
Lords	Westminster	0.02	7.45	2.49	64.53	53.12	2771
Norland	Kensington and Chelsea	0.0	7.18	3.71	56.90	47.16	1914
North Stanley	Kensington and Chelsea	-0.02	7.35	3.44	57.60	47.56	2151
Archway	Haringey	-0.03	8.11	3.74	51.42	44.70	2808
Cheyne	Kensington and Chelsea	-0.05	8.26	2.91	58.01	46.63	2267
Vanbrugh	Greenwich	-0.05	8.21	3.05	63.43	43.24	2390
Brentford Clifden	Hounslow	-0.08	7.06	4.59	50.65	43.90	3058
Abbey Wood	Greenwich	-0.11	8.32	3.86	42.38	46.78	2902
Ravenor	Ealing	-0.20	8.43	4.59	52.80	35.26	4299
Horniman	Lewisham	-0.28	8.27	3.64	52.35	40.05	3897
Thurlow Park	Lambeth	-0.28	8.30	3.23	52.03	43.02	2852
Avery Hill	Greenwich	-0.33	8.48	2.49	60.90	43.28	1363
Silver Street	Enfield	-0.33	8.59	4.95	38.28	38.42	2649
Arnos	Enfield	-0.35	7.00	5.28	41.40	41.51	3145
Alperton	Brent	-0.37	7.25	9.54	23.48	38.54	2896
Abbey	Merton	-0.38	6.97	3.39	45.28	50.80	3690
Fortis Green	Haringey	-0.39	8.29	3.27	50.13	41.92	3788
Wood End	Hillingdon	-0.39	6.94	6.50	49.70	32.18	2513
Beddington South	Sutton	-0.41	7.77	2.88	64.71	40.31	3434
Coldharbour	Greenwich	-0.45	8.53	2.19	75.69	38.50	2324
Bridge	Redbridge	-0.45	8.23	3.80	44.69	40.66	4366
Palace	Hammersmith and Fulham	-0.49	8.21	3.32	45.20	43.09	2321
Hampstead Town	Camden	-0.50	8.44	3.56	47.92	38.87	2256
Cambridge Road	Enfield	-0.54	7.78	3.49	54.42	38.32	3041
Mandeville	Ealing	-0.56	6.86	5.01	52.04	34.87	4222
Cowley	Hillingdon	-0.57	7.70	3.64	60.38	34.88	3150
South Norwood	Croydon	-0.58	7.48	3.93	43.91	41.53	4787
Golders Green	Barnet	-0.58	7.84	5.04	37.50	37.85	5224
Richmond Town	Richmond Upon Thames	-0.58	6.36	3.16	50.57	49.34	2978

Ranking of GLC Wards on a Multiple Deprivation Index, Calculated from 4 Indicators

Ward Name	Borough	Zscore Index	Unemployment	Overcrowding	Renting	No Car	Total H'holds
Kenton East	Harrow	-0.60	7.21	7.22	33.58	34.20	3392
Hainault	Redbridge	-0.61	8.50	2.70	56.87	38.91	3673
Streatham South	Lambeth	-0.63	8.30	4.94	30.56	40.59	4103
Hillingdon	Hillingdon	-0.65	7.74	3.96	49.03	36.46	2474
Greenhill	Harrow	-0.66	7.42	4.32	37.45	42.25	3172
Ordnance	Enfield	-0.67	7.38	4.88	38.61	38.48	4017
Gladstone	Brent	-0.69	8.51	7.24	23.04	36.12	2556
Yeading	Hillingdon	-0.69	7.38	6.23	43.38	30.46	2409
Bowes	Enfield	-0.70	8.54	5.84	25.42	38.91	2860
Greatfield	Newham	-0.70	7.41	4.55	32.74	43.86	4084
Upper Norwood	Croydon	-0.72	6.94	4.34	47.81	37.46	3039
Grove	Kingston Upon Thames	-0.72	7.04	3.02	48.47	45.39	3495
Muswell Hill	Haringey	-0.78	7.48	3.36	47.39	40.22	4193
Eastbrook	Barking and Dagenham	-0.79	7.60	4.22	47.06	34.67	3283
Mortlake	Richmond Upon Thames	-0.79	6.35	3.22	53.01	43.94	3505
Perry Hill	Lewisham	-0.80	7.88	3.19	41.60	42.65	4233
Woodhouse	Barnet	-0.82	7.01	4.43	41.99	38.22	5328
Frognal	Camden	-0.83	7.13	4.73	50.14	32.33	2136
Belgrave	Westminster	-0.86	4.65	3.80	65.30	43.81	2343
Valley	Waltham Forest	-0.86	8.22	4.79	32.29	37.04	4178
Thornton Heath	Croydon	-0.89	6.84	4.34	36.87	41.70	5001
St. Alphege	Enfield	-0.91	7.17	4.98	36.77	36.64	2630
Airfield	Havering	-0.92	7.61	4.90	45.20	30.89	3491
Marlborough	Harrow	-0.193	7.18	5.49	29.19	39.42	3244
Cray	Bexley	-0.94	8.99	3.24	47.33	33.06	2079
Graveney	Merton	-0.95	7.56	5.70	22.79	42.46	1966
Wealdstone	Harrow	-0.95	6.48	6.03	32.23	37.71	3183
Feltham Central	Hounslow	-1.00	6.77	4.29	46.75	35.13	3660
Knightsbridge	Westminster	-1.02	6.63	3.07	56.89	38.17	1661

Ward	Borough						
Lawrie Park & Kent	Bromley	-1.11	7.60	2.85	42.12	41.31	3609
Roe Green	Brent	-1.11	7.65	7.32	23.82	32.89	2611
Beulah	Croydon	-1.12	8.45	5.41	33.06	29.83	3237
College	Southwark	-1.12	6.88	3.29	56.12	34.51	3860
Aldborough	Redbridge	-1.13	7.71	3.63	39.04	36.96	4211
Alexandra	Haringey	-1.16	7.87	3.87	37.40	35.55	3537
Stanmore South	Harrow	-1.16	7.84	7.07	21.96	33.89	3466
Bush Hill	Enfield	-1.21	6.79	3.15	40.11	42.59	3204
Fryent	Brent	-1.22	6.73	6.05	30.73	33.92	3026
Orpington Central	Bromley	-1.24	7.19	5.22	39.81	29.85	3527
Addiscombe	Croydon	-1.27	6.31	2.82	38.24	48.50	5565
Fairfield	Croydon	-1.28	6.30	3.01	45.02	42.21	6280
West Thornton	Croydon	-1.29	6.41	5.47	26.96	39.79	5011
Pollards Hill	Merton	-1.30	7.20	3.61	45.27	33.61	3245
Heathrow	Hillingdon	-1.30	5.98	5.33	53.29	27.97	2475
Feltham North	Hounslow	-1.31	5.75	4.80	47.09	33.20	3697
Green Street	Enfield	-1.32	7.19	4.14	37.44	34.71	3408
Isleworth North	Hounslow	-1.32	5.79	3.98	43.43	38.73	3698
Hatch Lane	Waltham Forest	-1.34	7.17	2.72	44.06	39.66	4376
Richmond Hill	Richmond Upon Thames	-1.35	6.88	2.09	54.56	41.09	3686
Figge's March	Merton	-1.36	6.48	4.04	40.18	36.08	3539
Waxlow	Ealing	-1.37	7.32	9.69	18.67	29.64	3920
St. Mary Cray	Bromley	-1.37	6.84	3.76	44.57	33.67	5508
Crane	Hillingdon	-1.37	7.36	5.36	33.85	30.23	2446
Trinity	Merton	-1.38	5.90	3.20	39.40	44.90	3089
Belvedere	Bexley	-1.39	6.90	4.61	31.42	36.43	4102
Jubilee	Enfield	-1.40	7.03	4.67	26.52	39.41	2892
East Bedfont	Hounslow	-1.40	6.29	4.38	52.65	29.36	4184
Seven Kings	Redbridge	-1.41	8.07	4.31	25.22	37.83	3783
St. Pauls	Barnet	-1.42	6.66	4.59	31.44	37.23	5446
Bensham Manor	Croydon	-1.44	6.49	5.07	24.73	41.12	4969
Clementswood	Redbridge	-1.45	7.57	5.81	20.16	37.43	4042
Hillside	Merton	-1.45	6.78	2.39	44.87	42.19	3811
Blythe Hill	Lewisham	-1.48	6.47	3.34	39.78	38.88	2637

Ranking of GLC Wards on a Multiple Deprivation Index, Calculated from 4 Indicators

Ward Name	Borough	Zscore Index	Unemployment	Overcrowding	Renting	No Car	Total H'holds
Ham & Petersham	Richmond Upon Thames	-1.48	7.37	3.30	50.47	30.35	3089
Chiswick Riverside	Hounslow	-1.50	7.03	2.47	49.85	37.07	3769
West Drayton	Hillingdon	-1.55	7.16	4.70	41.76	27.55	2323
Ashburton	Croydon	-1.58	6.51	3.58	37.96	36.84	3153
Canbury	Kingston Upon Thames	-1.58	6.49	2.65	40.20	42.22	3134
Barnhill	Hillingdon	-1.59	6.12	5.91	35.37	29.66	3483
Surbiton Hill	Kingston Upon Thames	-1.60	5.97	2.63	45.17	41.88	3268
Hendon	Barnet	-1.62	6.26	3.50	40.98	36.25	6000
Chapel End	Waltham Forest	-1.62	6.12	3.35	33.69	42.67	4242
Barnes	Richmond Upon Thames	-1.66	6.91	2.49	46.56	36.73	3812
Roxbourne	Harow	-1.66	6.03	5.14	31.24	34.47	3483
St. Mark's	Kingston Upon Thames	-1.67	5.96	2.99	41.43	40.24	3657
Brooklands	Havering	-1.68	7.08	3.40	31.28	38.47	2880
Slade	Greenwich	-1.69	6.33	2.58	38.44	43.02	2672
Kingsbury	Brent	-1.70	6.65	4.55	35.79	31.06	2858
Rylands	Croydon	-1.72	6.10	3.01	34.81	42.82	3094
Woodside	Croydon	-1.74	6.21	4.16	29.64	38.33	2982
Martins Hill & Tow	Bromley	-1.75	5.61	2.68	43.19	30.91	3156
Feltham South	Hounslow	-1.75	5.97	4.47	41.19	30.91	3156
Finchley	Barnet	-1.76	6.97	3.87	34.80	32.82	5143
Hanger Lane	Ealing	-1.79	6.97	3.25	37.24	34.42	4801
Highgate	Haringey	-1.79	5.89	2.90	48.61	35.76	2483
Catford	Lewisham	-1.88	6.26	2.46	39.86	40.54	2963
Sutton East	Sutton	-1.89	5.39	3.11	42.62	38.58	2994
St. Mildred	Lewisham	-1.90	7.01	2.69	38.44	35.75	4165
Durnsford	Merton	-1.93	6.53	3.43	26.90	40.68	2171
Bullsmoor	Enfield	-1.94	7.13	3.31	39.30	30.48	3509
Crayford	Bexley	-2.00	6.11	3.15	39.79	34.57	3785
Harefield	Hillingdon	-2.02	5.34	3.03	65.65	28.64	2230

Costons	Ealing	-2.07	6.19	6.09	22.34	31.82	3796
Dundonald	Merton	-2.13	5.45	2.98	29.48	44.79	3351
Northfield	Ealing	-2.14	5.69	3.41	28.23	41.08	4722
Arkley	Barnet	-2.14	5.14	3.28	48.51	32.61	5434
Well Hall	Greenwich	-2.14	5.11	2.36	42.09	42.83	2628
Norbury	Croydon	-2.15	6.54	3.38	29.20	35.93	4617
East Twickenham	Richmond Upon Thames	-2.15	6.26	1.89	41.38	40.92	4106
Queensbury	Brent	-2.17	6.51	7.10	17.67	30.65	2886
Fairlop	Redbridge	-2.21	7.31	3.31	28.02	33.22	3847
Ridgeway	Harrow	-2.23	5.95	4.20	26.68	34.95	3332
Kew	Richmond Upon Thames	-2.32	6.04	2.35	40.63	35.83	4174
Tarn	Greenwich	-2.36	6.93	2.11	36.57	35.53	1277
Edgware	Barnet	-2.36	7.70	3.19	33.46	27.49	5401
Preston	Brent	-2.38	6.74	3.71	24.76	33.66	4236
Heston East	Hounslow	-2.38	6.27	4.83	31.75	26.10	2362
Ruskin	Southwark	-2.39	6.12	1.70	46.66	37.15	3637
Harlington	Hillingdon	-2.43	5.57	4.63	34.41	27.58	3496
Palmers Green	Enfield	-2.45	6.29	2.97	26.08	38.20	3531
Pitshanger	Ealing	-2.54	6.04	3.09	33.11	32.17	4854
Harrow On The Hill	Harrow	-2.54	5.16	4.60	27.78	28.72	3917
Wood End	Ealing	-2.56	5.88	4.60	27.78	28.72	3917
Clock House	Bromley	-2.58	5.53	2.75	30.49	38.20	4145
South Hornchurch	Havering	-2.58	7.11	4.36	27.24	25.48	4199
Roxeth	Harrow	-2.61	5.68	4.81	22.00	32.61	3554
Chase	Enfield	-2.70	5.89	2.03	45.13	31.91	3335
Bromley Common & K	Bromley	-2.71	5.66	2.92	34.41	32.04	6091
Tolworth West	Kingston Upon Thames	-2.73	5.26	2.65	34.97	35.19	2185
Heston Central	Hounslow	-2.74	5.47	6.07	20.29	28.93	2173
Rayners Lane	Harrow	-2.79	5.82	4.35	22.68	31.06	3312
Clockhouse	Sutton	-2.81	6.31	2.85	53.79	21.60	751
Palewell	Richmond Upon Thames	-2.81	6.39	1.73	35.72	35.77	3530
Central Twickenham	Richmond Upon Thames	-2.81	5.78	2.52	30.45	35.48	2936
Northumberland Hea	Bexley	-2.84	5.85	3.06	26.80	33.69	3855
Hampton Wick	Richmond Upon Thames	-2.86	6.01	2.06	36.20	33.62	4044

Ranking of GLC Wards on a Multiple Deprivation Index, Calculated from 4 Indicators

Ward Name	Borough	Zscore Index	Unemployment	Overcrowding	Renting	No Car	Total H'holds
Fullwell	Redbridge	-2.86	6.43	2.46	31.17	31.81	4106
Wrythe Green	Sutton	-2.91	5.53	2.61	34.59	32.09	2723
Palace	Greenwich	-2.92	5.87	1.63	38.36	36.23	1228
Raynes Park	Merton	-2.95	5.00	1.98	40.24	35.97	3842
Snaresbrook	Redbridge	-2.96	6.38	1.52	34.68	36.53	3685
Plaistow & Sundrid	Bromley	-2.99	5.64	2.05	35.15	34.43	5517
East Wickham	Bexley	-3.03	5.96	2.50	30.38	32.03	3884
St. Edward's	Havering	-3.05	6.56	2.29	25.38	34.27	2530
St. Andrew	Lewisham	-3.06	6.23	2.20	24.32	37.39	2767
Sudbury	Brent	-3.07	6.11	4.19	19.76	29.83	2743
Blackheath	Greenwich	-3.10	5.43	1.74	41.64	33.19	2642
Teddington	Richmond Upon Thames	-3.14	5.07	1.93	35.21	36.42	4087
Canons	Harrow	-3.14	5.76	2.17	35.07	31.05	3273
Sutton Central	Sutton	-3.19	4.32	1.95	32.84	42.07	2661
Copers Cope	Bromley	-3.20	4.96	2.54	37.40	30.25	3382
Church Street	Enfield	-3.21	6.19	3.11	24.00	29.65	3283
Spring Park	Croydon	-3.21	5.82	3.69	30.13	24.59	3737
Cockfosters	Enfield	-3.23	5.83	1.74	35.28	33.08	3390
Tolworth South	Kingston Upon Thames	-3.27	5.84	2.89	23.63	32.02	1985
Headstone	Harrow	-3.31	5.30	3.94	20.59	31.03	3196
South Twickenham	Richmond Upon Thames	-3.34	5.29	2.17	32.57	32.34	3632
Friern Barnet	Barnet	-3.45	4.93	2.52	33.34	29.88	5270
Northwood Hills	Hillingdon	-3.45	4.64	1.75	40.26	33.49	3716
Sutton South	Sutton	-3.50	4.08	2.01	39.37	34.45	4036
Perivale	Ealing	-3.51	5.54	6.05	12.49	28.65	4363
East Barnet	Barnet	-3.52	5.38	2.44	30.70	29.04	5085
Chingford Green	Waltham Forest	-3.52	5.74	2.31	29.41	29.31	4325
Healthfield	Richmond Upon Thames	-3.57	4.61	3.04	31.72	27.97	3714
Hillingdeon North	Hillingdon	-3.57	5.90	3.31	25.93	24.69	2541

Coombe	Kingston Upon Thames	-3.60	5.52	2.86	38.22	21.99	1643
Bourne	Hillingdon	-3.61	4.16	2.57	39.15	28.71	2567
Mauney	Havering	-3.61	5.56	2.63	25.95	29.03	4251
Elm Park	Havering	-3.61	5.83	2.81	20.78	30.84	4278
Hylands	Havering	-3.62	5.58	2.75	21.45	31.62	4111
Cambridge	Kingston Upon Thames	-3.63	5.17	2.64	26.18	30.31	2953
Heath Park	Havering	3.63	5.58	2.55	22.77	31.64	3105
Mill Hill	Barnet	-3.65	5.15	2.27	33.59	28.10	5553
Hale End	Waltham Forest	-3.65	5.75	2.14	26.17	30.92	2667
Collier Row	Havering	-3.68	6.80	3.90	22.25	21.08	2664
Larkswood	Waltham Forest	-3.75	5.40	2.15	23.08	34.05	4364
Cranbrook	Redbridge	-3.72	6.00	2.60	19.90	31.04	3613
Village	Merton	-3.74	5.92	1.67	34.76	27.64	3055
Longthornton	Merton	-3.75	4.52	3.44	21.36	31.50	3431
Chadwell Heath	Barking and Dagenham	-3.78	5.05	2.25	24.82	32.91	3328
Hampton Nursery	Richmond Upon Thames	-3.78	5.21	3.49	30.47	22.16	1536
New Park	Enfield	-3.80	6.33	3.67	14.08	29.15	2671
Charville	Hillingdon	-3.81	5.44	4.34	23.05	22.01	3506
West Twickenham	Richmond Upon Thames	-3.84	4.61	2.00	27.35	34.47	2548
Hampton	Richmond Upon Thames	-3.84	4.25	2.50	34.12	28.60	3453
Hounslow South	Hounslow	-3.84	5.13	4.28	18.51	26.38	3458
Town	Enfield	-3.85	4.54	1.67	27.51	37.79	2992
Wallington North	Sutton	-3.86	4.44	2.00	29.63	33.53	3645
Harrow Weald	Harrow	-3.88	4.60	2.56	28.77	29.02	3518
St. Martins	Hillingdon	-3.89	4.65	2.05	33.47	29.31	2982
Stanmore Park	Harrow	-3.89	5.31	2.20	34.26	25.06	3456
Highfield	Enfield	-3.94	5.52	2.01	25.13	30.25	2881
Pinner	Harrow	-3.95	5.01	2.36	32.57	25.54	3559
Wallington	Sutton	-3.96	4.62	2.04	33.24	28.86	3535
Shrewsbury	Greenwich	-3.99	6.15	2.41	25.25	24.63	1204
Croham	Croydon	-4.01	5.26	1.80	26.28	31.49	4832
Hacton	Havering	-4.03	5.53	2.59	19.42	29.88	3826
Newbury	Redbridge	-4.04	6.40	2.92	12.78	31.77	3904
Beddington North	Sutton	-4.06	5.27	2.34	30.21	24.76	2271

Ranking of GLC Wards on a Multiple Deprivation Index, Calculated from 4 Indicators

Ward Name	Borough	Zscore Index	Indicators				Total H'holds
			Unemployment	Overcrowding	Renting	No Car	
Hale	Barnet	-4.07	5.58	2.85	22.98	25.07	4857
Longbridge	Barking and Dagenham	-4.08	4.99	1.52	26.21	34.54	3365
Church End	Redbridge	-4.09	4.47	1.87	28.30	32.56	3580
Hillingdon West	Hillingdon	-4.14	3.90	2.53	40.49	24.29	3080
West Barnes	Merton	-4.18	4.43	3.00	17.96	32.62	3468
Chessington North	Kingston Upon Thames	-4.18	4.59	2.29	21.36	26.09	1875
East Sheen	Richmond Upon Thames	-4.20	5.53	1.38	26.87	31.26	2456
Hampton Hill	Richmond Upon Thames	-4.23	4.96	1.57	31.57	28.87	3450
Burlington	Kingston Upon Thames	-4.24	4.05	2.39	21.82	34.37	2090
Upton	Bexley	-4.26	5.87	1.70	27.93	25.84	3648
Sidcup East	Bexley	-4.26	4.56	1.88	27.09	30.71	4090
Spring Grove	Hounslow	-4.27	5.16	2.48	22.86	26.78	3836
Totteridge	Barnet	-4.36	4.99	2.90	22.59	24.49	5680
Cannon Hill	Merton	-4.38	4.77	1.89	20.99	32.99	3288
St. Andrew's	Havering	-4.38	4.86	1.82	22.74	31.63	4275
Mayfield	Redbridge	-4.39	6.48	2.51	12.78	29.88	4227
Rainham	Havering	-4.40	6.17	3.95	14.07	22.65	4293
Sutcliffe	Greenwich	-4.41	4.50	1.77	26.84	30.37	1416
Centenary	Harrow	-4.41	5.05	3.83	14.15	26.91	3187
Garden Suburb	Barnet	-4.50	5.22	1.38	28.22	28.41	5297
Wanstead	Redbridge	-4.51	5.43	1.36	25.49	29.31	3452
Kenley	Croydon	-4.53	4.38	2.63	29.73	22.66	3162
Christchurch	Bexley	-4.57	5.13	1.41	19.19	35.03	3840
Eltham park	Greenwich	-4.58	4.94	1.50	25.48	29.48	2527
St. Michael's	Bexley	-4.62	4.88	2.60	17.10	28.47	3731
Kenton West	Harrow	-4.62	5.14	4.32	13.36	23.56	3331
Hook	Kingston Upon Thames	-4.63	3.92	2.46	26.67	26.38	1867
Norbiton Park	Kingston Upon Thames	-4.65	5.33	1.53	23.43	28.18	2091
Merton Park	Merton	-4.79	4.42	2.02	18.25	31.61	3118

Deansfield	Hillingdon	-4.82	4.76	2.62	22.54	22.62	2715
Barnhill	Brent	-4.83	5.05	1.98	25.32	23.17	2630
Endlebury	Waltham Forest	-4.84	5.37	1.75	20.76	26.36	2910
Willow	Enfield	-4.87	3.62	1.80	23.22	32.64	3436
Roding	Redbridge	-4.88	4.83	1.61	19.53	30.54	4112
Whitton	Richmond Upon Thames	-5.03	4.06	2.60	17.62	27.59	3382
Northwood	Hillingdon	-5.03	4.56	2.75	32.36	16.75	3130
Tudor	Kingston Upon Thames	-5.07	4.62	1.51	21.01	28.95	3241
New Eltham	Greenwich	-5.08	4.87	1.74	16.37	30.07	2645
Eden Park	Bromley	-5.17	4.27	1.52	21.65	28.95	3496
Hadley	Barnet	-5.18	4.74	1.69	20.73	26.05	6281
Chessington South	Kingston Upon Thames	-5.22	3.86	2.64	20.71	23.91	3230
Danson	Bexley	-5.24	4.78	1.77	14.70	30.45	3564
Eastcote	Hillingdon	-5.24	4.53	2.14	23.18	21.89	3823
Worchester Park Nor	Sutton	-5.25	3.76	2.56	17.42	27.27	3358
Sidcup West	Bexley	-5.43	3.68	1.16	26.16	29.36	3887
Cavendish	Hillingdon	-5.44	3.98	1.11	26.41	27.95	2522
Rosehill	Sutton	-5.47	4.37	1.69	18.48	26.65	2191
Uxbridge North	Hillingdon	-5.47	4.41	1.51	23.79	23.83	2047
Cranham East	Havering	-5.49	4.10	1.98	21.88	23.15	2683
Carshalton Central	Sutton	-5.51	3.54	1.47	22.80	28.91	2382
Sutton West	Sutton	-5.56	3.70	1.90	20.56	25.88	2155
Southgate Green	Enfield	-5.57	4.74	1.28	19.65	26.17	3358
Monks Orchard	Croydon	-5.57	4.70	1.68	21.31	22.17	3358
Harold Wood	Havering	-5.66	4.36	2.06	16.80	23.85	3520
Oakwood	Enfield	-5.70	3.83	1.55	18.46	28.12	3288
Chadwell	Redbridge	-5.71	4.81	2.23	10.88	26.94	3952
Darwin	Bromley	-5.73	6.02	1.80	25.84	14.60	1610
Winchmore Hill	Enfield	-5.74	4.17	1.73	18.17	24.80	3000
Sudbury Court	Brent	-5.74	4.37	2.90	12.49	22.93	2105
Hill	Kingston Upon Thames	-5.75	3.91	1.66	26.95	20.84	2052
Coulsdon East	Croydon	-5.88	3.94	2.06	24.02	19.01	4371
Brunswick Park	Barnet	-5.92	4.07	1.79	15.31	25.80	5022
Berrylands	Kingston Upon Thames	-5.96	4.20	1.21	20.32	24.85	3228

Ranking of GLC Wards on a Multiple Deprivation Index, Calculated from 4 Indicators

Ward Name	Borough	Zscore Index	Indicators				Total H'holds
			Unemployment	Overcrowding	Renting	No Car	
Purley	Croydon	-6.01	4.29	1.42	17.60	24.42	5018
Hayes	Bromley	-6.09	3.79	1.21	20.77	25.31	5552
Barkingside	Redbridge	-6.09	4.38	1.45	12.04	29.03	4545
Carshalton North	Sutton	-6.12	3.70	2.22	12.33	26.22	2570
St. James	Kingston Upon Thames	6.16	4.19	1.58	18.39	21.85	2599
Gidea Park	Havering	-6.16	5.14	1.39	14.03	23.19	2594
Bostall	Bexley	-6.21	4.08	2.12	10.23	26.87	3579
Brampton	Bexley	-6.22	4.02	1.60	12.48	27.68	3815
Wemborough	Harrow	-6.22	4.45	2.55	12.29	20.36	3377
Cheam West	Sutton	-6.23	3.59	1.53	15.56	26.88	2153
Chelsfield & Goddi	Bromley	-6.30	5.00	1.53	18.62	18.09	5182
Chislehurst	Bromley	-6.33	4.44	1.27	19.12	20.99	5681
Sutton Common	Sutton	-6.33	3.68	2.08	11.83	25.69	2257
Bush Hill South	Enfield	-6.37	4.44	1.59	11.25	25.76	2773
Lower Morden	Merton	-6.40	3.26	1.87	13.81	26.36	3368
Lamorbey	Bexley	-6.42	4.01	1.68	12.64	24.82	3514
Barnehurst North	Bexley	-6.42	4.06	1.35	12.28	27.70	1482
Kelsey Park	Bromley	-6.46	4.26	0.65	19.91	25.59	3370
Barnehurst	Bexley	-6.48	4.06	1.45	13.67	24.54	2282
Manor	Hillingdon	-6.52	3.02	2.29	10.68	28.01	2790
Ruislip	Hillingdon	-6.56	3.80	1.86	21.47	16.90	2361
Hatch End	Harrow	-6.60	3.90	1.12	20.16	21.36	3224
Belmont	Sutton	-6.65	3.82	1.02	17.88	23.73	2550
Heathfield	Croydon	-6.71	3.96	2.26	19.40	14.88	4392
Grange	Enfield	-6.72	4.25	0.83	16.54	24.06	3482
Blackfen	Bexley	-6.75	4.21	1.78	8.78	25.78	2415
Rise Park	Havering	-6.86	4.28	1.91	11.62	19.70	2770
Kenton	Brent	-6.88	4.37	1.37	13.93	20.19	2928
Carshalton Beeches	Sutton	-6.94	4.00	1.44	16.36	18.70	3056

Deanfield	Greenwich	-6.95	3.45	2.11	7.20	28.11	1277
Sanderstead	Croydon	-6.99	3.84	1.50	20.10	16.39	3528
Bickley	Bromley	-7.03	4.20	0.90	15.15	22.07	4784
West	Enfield	-7.04	4.37	1.60	19.42	14.35	3614
Clayhall	Redbridge	-7.05	4.54	1.05	10.81	23.78	4476
St. Mary's	Bexley	-7.09	3.80	1.50	13.22	20.52	4008
Ardleigh Green	Havering	-7.23	3.40	1.97	13.24	18.52	2893
Tolworth East	Kingston Upon Thames	-7.25	3.74	1.63	10.88	21.08	1930
Headstone North	Harrow	-7.32	4.38	1.11	12.15	20.12	3341
Pinner West	Harrow	-7.44	3.56	0.82	15.37	21.88	3409
Blendon & Penhill	Bexley	-7.55	4.29	1.81	6.99	20.72	3490
Monkhams	Redbridge	-7.64	3.95	1.09	14.37	17.56	3569
North Cheam	Sutton	-7.66	3.40	2.76	5.78	21.18	2352
Worcester Park Sou	Sutton	-7.67	3.10	1.46	9.60	23.38	2197
Woodcote & Coulsdo	Croydon	-7.68	3.28	1.25	15.67	17.82	4717
Shortlands	Bromley	-7.88	3.66	0.77	12.99	20.46	3627
Upminster	Havering	-7.94	3.63	1.02	9.19	22.31	4017
West Wickham South	Bromley	-8.17	3.03	0.80	12.81	20.91	3638
Petts Wood & Knoll	Bromley	-8.30	2.97	0.96	11.39	20.33	5620
Ickenham	Hillingdon	-8.44	3.38	1.09	12.75	15.54	3773
Malden Manor	Kingston Upon Thames	-8.45	3.06	0.83	10.50	20.72	1800
Falconwood	Bexley	-8.76	3.25	2.14	2.44	25.44	1309
Emerson Park	Havering	-8.80	4.26	1.29	6.05	16.27	3175
Crofton	Bromley	-8.91	2.57	1.14	9.76	18.16	3769
West Wickham North	Bromley	-9.12	3.07	0.56	10.02	18.52	3262
Farnborough	Bromley	-9.40	3.20	1.06	7.82	15.03	2839
Biggin Hill	Bromley	-9.98	3.06	2.01	9.90	7.90	3547
Woodcote	Sutton	-9.98	4.79	0.75	14.49	6.64	1070
Cheam South	Sutton	-10.68	2.85	0.62	8.86	11.03	1942
Selsdon	Croydon	-10.82	2.63	0.55	6.73	13.47	3475
Cranham West	Havering	-11.01	3.16	0.87	4.09	12.42	2543

References

ARMSTRONG, B. (1984) '1981 Census: Ward & Borough Indices for Greater London', GLC Statistical Series No. 30, Greater London Council.

ARMSTRONG, H.W. (1978) 'Community Regional Policy: A Survey & a Critique,' *Regional Studies*, Vol. 12

ARONSON, N. (1984) 'The Making of the U.S. Bureau of Labor Statistics Family Budget Series: Relativism and the Rhetoric of Subsistence,' Department of Sociology, Northwestern University, Evanston, Illinois.

BECKERMAN, E. *et al.* (1979) *Poverty and the impact of income maintenance programmes*, International Labour Office, Geneva.

BENTHAM, C.G. (1980) 'A Classification of Local Authorities in the UK Inner Urban Areas Act 1978', *Environment and Planning* 1980 Vol. 12.

BERKMAN, L. and SYME, S.L. (1979) 'Social Networks, Host Resistance and Mortality: A Nine Year Follow-Up Study of Alameda County Residents', *American Journal of Epidemiology*, Vol. 109.

BERTHOUD, R. (1976) 'The Disadvantages of Inequality: A Study of Social Deprivation', a PEP Report, MacDonald and Jane's, London.

BERTHOUD, R. and BROWN, J.C., with COOPER, S. (1980) *Poverty and the Development of Anti-Poverty Policy: The United Kingdom*, Policy Studies Institute, London.

BEVERIDGE REPORT (1942) *Social Insurance and Allied Services*, Cmd. 6064, HMSO, London.

BLACK REPORT (1980) 'Inequalities in Health', Report of a Working Group, DHSS, London.

BOOTH (1886) 'Occupations of the People of the United Kingdom, 1801-1881,' *Journal of the Royal Statistical Society*.

BOOTH, C. (1902-3) *Life and Labour of the People in London*, (3rd edition), MacMillan, London.

BRANDT, W. (Chairman) (1980) *North-South: A Programme for Survival*, Pan Books, London.

BROADHEAD, W.E. *et al.* (1983) 'The Epidemiological Evidence for a Relationship Between Social Support and Health', *American Journal of Epidemiology*, Vol. 117.

BROWN, JOAN (1981) 'Policies to Combat Poverty', Annex VII to Chapter IV of the Commission's Final Report to the Council on the First Programme of Pilot Schemes and Studies to Combat Poverty, Commission of the European Communities, Brussels.

BROWN, M. and MADGE, N. (1982) *Despite the Welfare State*, Heinemann Educational Books, London.

BULMER, M. (1984) 'Local Inequality: Sociability, Isolation and Loneliness as Factors in the Differential Provision of Neighbourhood Care', paper presented to the Social Administration Association conference, University of Kent.

CENTRAL STATISTICAL OFFICE (1985) *Social Trends*, HMSO, London.

CHAMPION, A.G. and GREEN, A.E. (1985) 'In Search of Britain's Booming Towns: An Index of Local Economic Performance for Britain', Discussion Paper No. 72, Centre for Urban and Regional Development Studies, University of Newcastle upon Tyne.

CHARLTON, J.R.H., HARTLEY, R.M., SILVER, R., and HOLLAND, W.W. (1983) 'Geographical Variation in Mortality from Conditions Amenable to Medical Intervention in England and Wales', *The Lancet*, 1, pp.691-696.

COMMISSION OF THE EUROPEAN COMMUNITIES (1981) *Final Report from the First Programme of Pilot Schemes and Studies to Combat Poverty*, Brussels.

CONGDON, P. (1984) 'Social Structure in the London Boroughs: Evidence from the 1981 Census & Changes since 1971', Statistical Series No. 50, Greater London Council.

COOK, D.G. and SHAPER, A.G. (1984) 'Unemployment and Health' in Harrington, M. (ed) *Recent Advances in Occupational Health II*.

COULTER, J. (1978) 'Grid Square Census Data as a Source for the Study of Deprivation in British Conurbations', Working Paper 13, Census Research Unit, Durham University.

DAVIES, H. (1984) '1981 Census — A Ward Index of Deprivation', GLC Statistical Series No. 35, Greater London Council.

DEPARTMENT OF THE ENVIRONMENT (1975a) 'Housing Act 1974: Renewal Strategies', Circular 13?75, HMSO, London.

DEPARTMENT OF THE ENVIRONMENT (1975b) 'Housing Act 1974: Parts IV, V and VI, Housing Action Areas, Priority Neighbourhoods and General Improvement Areas', Circular 14/75, HMSO, London.

DEPARTMENT OF THE ENVIRONMENT (1983) 'Urban Deprivation', Information Note No. 2, Inner Cities Directorate, Department of the Environment, London.

DEPARTMENT OF PLANNING AND DESIGN, SHEFFIELD (1983) 'Areas of Poverty in Sheffield', Report to Urban Strategy Panel, Supporting Technical Review of Priority Areas of Deprivation-Methodology, Sheffield.

DESAI, M. & SHAH, A. (1985) 'An Econometric Approach to the Measurement of Poverty', Welfare State Programme No. 2., Suntory Toyota International Centre for Economics and Related Disciplines, London School of Economics.

DESAI, M. (1986) 'On Defining the Poverty Threshold', in Golding P. (ed) *Excluding the Poor*, Child Poverty Action Group, London.

DILNOT, A.W., KAY, J.A. & MORRIS, C.N. (1984) *The Reform of Social Security*, Institute for Fiscal Studies, The Clarendon Press, Oxford.

DREWNOWSKI, J. and SCOTT, W. (1966) *The Level of Living Index*, Report No. 4, Research Institute of Social Development, United Nations, Geneva.

EVERSLEY, D. and BEGG, I. (1984) 'Deprivation in the Inner City — Social Indicators from the 1981 Census', ESRC, London.

FENDLER, C. and ORSHANSKY, M. (1979) 'Improving the Poverty Definition', Proceedings of the Social Statistics Section of the American Statistical Association.

FERGE, Z. and MILLER, S.M. (eds) (1987) *The Dynamics of Deprivation: A Cross-National Study*, for the European Centre for Social Welfare Training and Research, Vienna, Gower Press, London.

London.

FIELDS, G.S. (1980) *Poverty, Inequality and Development*, Cambridge University Press, Cambridge.

FIEGHEN, G.C., LANSLEY, P.S. and SMITH, A.D. (1977), *Poverty and Progress in Britain, 1953-1973*, National Institute of Economic and Social Research, London.

FOX, A.J., and LEON, D.A. (1985) 'Mortality and Deprivation: Evidence from the OPCS Longitudinal Study', Social Statistics Research Unit Working Paper No. 33, City University, London.

GLC (1984) *The West London Report*, Greater London Council.

GLC (1985) *West London: The Public Enquiry into Jobs and Industry*, Greater London Council.

GLC (1985) 'Low Incomes in London: Evidence from the Family Expenditure Survey', Reviews & Studies Series No. 20, Greater London Council.

GLC (1985) *London Industrial Strategy*, Greater London Council.

GLC (1985) *Inner City Policy for London: A Fresh Approach*, Greater London Council.

GLC (1986) *The London Financial Strategy*, Greater London Council.

GLC (1986) *The London Labour Plan*, Greater London Council.

GHAI, D.P., et al. (1977) *The basic needs approach to development: some issues regarding concepts and methodology*, International Labour Office, Geneva.

GHAI, D., GODFREY, M., and LISK, F. (1979) *Planning for Basic Needs in Kenya*, International Labour Office, Geneva.

GOUGH, I. (1981) 'Poverty in the United Kingdom', *International Journal of Health Services*, 11 (2).

HAYES, M.G. (1986) 'Urban Decline and Deprivation: 1. Liverpool's Relative Position, a Technical Study', City Planning Department, Liverpool.

HAYTER, T. (1981) *The Creation of World Poverty*, Pluto Press, London.

HILLS, C and HOLLIS, J. (1986) 'Greater London Lifetables — 1979-82' GLC Statistical Series No. 35, Greater London Council.

HIMMELFART, G. (1984) *The Idea of Poverty: England in the Early Industrial Age*, Faber and Faber, London.

HOFFMAN, A., and LEIBFRIED, S. (1980) *Regularities in the History of Subsistence Scales — 100 Years of Tradition and the Deutscher Verein*, Research Centre on Social Movements and Social Policy, University of Bremen.

HOLTERMAN, S. (1975) 'Areas of Deprivation in Great Britain: An Analysis of 1971 Census Data', *Social Trends* 6, p.43.

HOOGEVELT, A.M.M. (1982) *The Third World in Global Development*, Macmillan, London.

INDIA (1978), *Five Year Plan 1978-83*, Planning Commission, Government of India, Dehli.

INNER LONDON CONSULTATIVE EMPLOYMENT GROUP (1986), *London's Labour Market 1965-1985*.

INTERNATIONAL LABOUR OFFICE (1976) *Employment Growth and Basic Needs: a One-World Problem*, Report of the Director General of the ILO, International Labour Office, Geneva.

INTERNATIONAL LABOUR OFFICE (1977) *Meeting Basic Needs: Strategies for Eradicating Mass Poverty and Unemployment*, conclusions of the World Employment Conference 1976,

International Labour Office, Geneva.

INTERNATIONAL LABOUR OFFICE (1984) *Into the Twenty-First Century:* The Development of Social Security, ILO, Geneva.

JANLERT, U. (1982) 'Unemployment and Health', background paper to WHO workshop on Health Policy in Relation to Unemployment in the Community, Leeds.

JARMAN, B. (1983) 'Identification of Underprivileged Areas', *British Medical Journal*, Vol. 2986, p.1705.

JARMAN, B. (1984) 'Underprivileged Areas: Validation and Distribution of Scores', *British Medical Journal*, Vol. 289, p.1587.

JOFFE, M. (1985) 'The Health Effects of Control Over Your Own Work — A Review of the Scientific Literature', for the Greater London Council, London.

LIEBFRIED, S. (1982) 'Existenzminimum und Fursorge-Richtsatze in der Weimarer Republik', *Jahrbuch der Sozialarbeit*, 4.

LIEBFRIED, S. & TENNSTEDT F. (eds) (1985) *Regulating Poverty and the Splitting of the German Welfare State*, Suhrkamp, Frankfurt/Main.

LLEWELLYN-SMITH, H. (ed) (1932) *New Survey of London Life and Labour*, MacMillan, London.

LONSDALE S. and WALKER, A. (1984) *A Right to Work: Disability and Employment*, Disability Alliance and Low Pay Unit, London.

MAASDORP, G. and HUMPHREYS, A.S.V. (eds) (1975) *From Shanty Town to Township: an economic study of African poverty and rehousing in a South African city*, Juta, Cape Town.

MACK, J. and LANSLEY, S. (1984) *Poor Britain*, Allen and Unwin, London.

MALAYSIA (1976) *Third Malaysia Plan 1976-1980*, Government Press Kuala Lumpur.

MARMOT, M.G., ADELSTEIN, A.M., ROBINSON, N. and ROSE, G. (1978) 'Changing Social Class Distribution of Heart Disease', *British Medical Journal* 2, p.1109-1112.

MARMOT, M.G. and McDOWALL, M.E. (1986) 'Mortality Decline and Widening Social Inequalities', *The Lancet* 2, pp.274-276.

MILLAR, A. (1980) 'A Study of Multiply Deprived Households in Scotland', Central Research Unit Papers, Scottish Office.

MINFORD, P.L. (1984) 'State Expenditure: A Study of Waste', Supplement to *Economic Affairs*.

MOSER, K.A., FOX, A.J., and JONES, D.R. (1984) 'Unemployment and Mortality in the OPCS Longitudinal Study', *The Lancet*, p.1324.

MURRAY, R. (1985) 'London and the GLC: Restructuring the Capital of Capital', *IDS Bulletin*, Vol. 16, No. 1, Institute of Development Studies, Sussex.

OECD (1976) *Public Expenditure on Income Maintenance and Programmes*, Studies in Resources Allocation No. 3, OECD, Paris.

PARLIAMENTARY SPOKESMAN'S WORKING GROUP (1983) *Alternative Regional Strategy*, Labour Party, London.

PIACHAUD, D. (1981) 'Peter Townsend and the Holy Grail', *New Society*, 10 September.

PILLAY, P.N. (1973) 'A Poverty Datum Line Study Among Africans in Durban', Occasional Paper No. 3., Department of Economics, University of Nepal.

PLATT, S. (1982) 'Unemployment and Suicide', *Unemployment Unit Bulletin* No. 6, p.4.

PLATT, S. (1984) 'Unemployment and Suicidal Behaviour: A Review of the Literature', *Social Science and Medicine* 19, 2, p.93.

REDFERN, P. (1982) 'Profile of our Cities', *Population Trends* No. 30.

REIN, M. (1970) 'Problems in the Definition and Measurement of Poverty' in Townsend, P. (ed) (1970).

ROWNTREE, B.S. (1901) *Poverty: A Study of Town Life*, Macmillan, London.

ROWNTREE, B.S. (1918, new edition 1937) *The Human Needs of Labour* Longmans, London.

SCOTT-SAMUEL, A. (1983) 'Identification of Underprivileged Areas', *British Medical Journal* 287, p.130.

SEN, A. (1983) 'Poor Relatively Speaking', *Oxford Economic Papers*, 35, p.153.

SEN, A. (1985), 'A Reply', *Oxford Economic Papers*, 37, p.669.

SMITH, A. (1812) *An Inquiry into the Natural Causes of the Wealth of Nations*, Ward, Lock (first published 1776), London.

STEDMAN-JONES (1971) *Outcast London*, Oxford.

THUNHURST, C. (1983) 'A Review of Priority Areas of Deprivation — Methodology', Areas of Poverty in Sheffield, 1983, Report to Urban Strategy Panel, Sheffield.

THUNHURST, C. (1985a) 'The Analysis of Small Area Statistics and Planning for Health', *The Statistician* 34, p.93.

THUNHURST, C. (1985b) 'Poverty and Health in the City of Sheffield', for the Environmental Health Department, Sheffield City Council, Sheffield.

TOWNSEND, P. (ed) (1970) *The Concept of Poverty*, Heinemann, London.

TOWNSEND, P. (1979) *Poverty in the United Kingdom*, Penguin Books, Harmondworth, Middlesex.

TOWNSEND, P. (1984a) 'A Theory of Poverty and the Role of Social Policy' in Loney, M. (ed) *Social Policy and Social Welfare*, Open University Press, Milton Keynes.

TOWNSEND, P. (1984b) 'Understanding Poverty and Inequality in Europe', in Walker, R., Lawson, R., and Townsend, P.,(eds.) *Responses to Poverty: Lessons from Europe*, Heinemann, London.

TOWNSEND, P. (1985) 'A Sociological Approach to the Measurement of Poverty — A Rejoinder to Professor Amartya Sen', *Oxford Economic Papers* 37, p.659.

TOWNSEND, P. (1987) 'Poverty in Europe', in Ferge, Z. and Miller, S.M. (eds).

TOWNSEND, P. (1987) 'Conceptualising Poverty', in Ferge, Z. and Miller, S.M. (eds).

TOWNSEND, P., PHILLIMORE, P., and BEATTIE, A. (1986) 'Inequalities in Health in the Northern Region: An Interim Report', Northern Regional Health Authority and the University of Bristol, Newcastle and Bristol.

TOWNSEND, P., SIMPSON, D., and TIBBS, N (1984) 'Inequalities of Health in the City of Bristol', Department of Social Administration, University of Bristol, Bristol.

UNESCO (1978) *Study in depth on the concept of basic human needs in relation to various ways of life and its possible implications for the action of the organisations*, UNESCO, Paris.

UNITED STATES DEPARTMENT OF HEALTH, EDUCATION AND

WELFARE (1976) *The Measure of Poverty,* a report to Congress as mandated by the Education Amendments of 1974.

WALKER, A (1982) 'The Social Consequences of Early Retirement', *Political Quarterly,* Vol. 53.

WALKER, A (1985) 'Early Retirement: Release & Refuge from the Labour Market', *The Quarterly Journal of Social Affairs,* Vol. 1, No. 3.

WARR, P., BANKS, M., and ULLAH, P. (1985) 'The Experience of Unemployment Among Black and White Urban Teenagers', *British Journal of Psychology* 76, 84-5.

WATKINS, S.J. (1982) 'Recession and Health — A Literature Review'.

WHITEFORD, P. (1985) 'A Family's Needs: Equivalence Scales, Poverty and Social Security', Research Paper No. 27, Development Division, Department of Social Security, Melbourne, Australia.

WILKINSON, R.G. (1986) 'Income and Mortality' in Wilkinson, R.G. (ed) *Class and Health: Research and Longitudinal Data,* for the ESRC, Tavistock, London. (ed) Class and Health: Research and Longitudinal Data, for the ESRC, Tavistock, London.